Raising
Babies

Also by Steve Biddulph

The Complete Secrets of Happy Children
The Secret of Happy Parents
Raising Boys
Manhood
Teaching About Youth Unemployment
Stories of Manhood
Love, Laughter and Parenting

Steve Biddulph

Raising Babies

Should
under 3s go to
nursery?

HarperThorsons
An Imprint of HarperCollins*Publishers*
77–85 Fulham Palace Road,
Hammersmith, London W6 8JB

The website address is: www.thorsonselement.com

and *HarperThorsons* are trademarks of
HarperCollins*Publishers* Ltd

First published by HarperThorsons 2006

A catalogue record of this book is
available from the British Library

ISBN-13 978-0-00-722192-9

Mixed Sources
Product group from well-managed
forests and other controlled sources
www.fsc.org Cert no. SW-COC-001806
© 1996 Forest Stewardship Council

FSC is a non-profit international organisation established to promote the
responsible management of the world's forests. Products carrying the FSC
label are independently certified to assure consumers that they come
from forests that are managed to meet the social, economic and
ecological needs of present and future generations.

Find out more about HarperCollins and the environment at
www.harpercollins.co.uk/green

Contents

Appendix

Introduction

This story begins 30 years ago. I was a young psychologist, just starting out, and I was sitting at my desk at around nine in the morning when the phone rang. The caller, a young woman, was in tears. For a moment or two I couldn't make out who she was, but I soon realized it was a friend – a social worker who had recently become the mother of a baby boy.

She was calling from her office. It was her first day back at work after four months of maternity leave, and she was very upset. She had just left her baby son for the first time, in a day nursery a couple of miles away from her workplace. This had always been the plan, long before her baby was born. But the baby had been acutely distressed to be left with strangers, and now she was distressed too, unable to concentrate on her work. She was worried that she was making a terrible mistake.

So we talked the problem over. I knew that most people would have said something to her like: 'Don't worry! I'm sure your baby is fine now. The staff are used to handling babies. He'll be happy and content when you go to pick him up', or some similar combination of reassuring platitudes. But I didn't say any of this. I asked her to tell me more about the situation. What she told me was revealing, and shocking in a way, but a tale that has come to be familiar as I talk to young parents all over the world.

As with most women (and many men too), my friend's decision to go back to work was made amid a tangle of other people's needs and expectations. Most of her friends had given birth to their babies, put them into nurseries at three, six or twelve months, and gone back to full-time work. It was the normal thing for her peer group, and it had simply been expected of her too. Her husband also wanted her back at work; they needed the money if they were to keep on track with their financial plans. Her boss wanted her back in the saddle as quickly as possible; she was a valued worker. However, there was something missing from this whole picture. What did *she* want? Somehow the most important question of all had not been asked – let alone answered!

What my friend was experiencing wasn't just the panic of being away from her baby for the first time in his life. It felt wrong to her in a deep way, and she realized she had been dreading this day. She had spent the last four months engrossed in her baby, finding her new role challenging, but also surprisingly and deeply rewarding. She did not want to miss out on the special and precious time when her little boy seemed so full of life, and was developing so quickly. It wasn't just her own needs, she knew she was the centre of this little baby's universe; it felt like a betrayal to leave him screaming in despair and walk away. Her modern ideas of independence were suddenly at war with deeper, newly aroused feelings and thoughts about what was important in life.

As we talked on, these feelings did not go away. In fact, they gained strength as her emotions, values and thinking all began to line up. In the end, she decided to request a meeting with her boss that same day and discuss a different course of action. In the end she took a further 18 months off and after that only returned to work part-time. She was deeply happy and relieved. And she was also lucky to have a good employer, a supportive partner and sufficient income to be able to make this choice.

· · ·

In the three decades that followed, I watched the use of full-time day nursery care for very young infants and toddlers increase dramatically in many countries around the world. I also visited many nurseries and daycare centres in person, and observed close-up the lives that little children had there, and the working conditions and feelings of the staff.

I had started out as a believer in the ideal of quality nursery care, and the role it played in allowing women to broaden their lives. (Like everyone else, I didn't question the role of men.) But the more I saw of the reality of daycare centres and nurseries, and the more conversations I had with parents and carers, the clearer it became to me that the reality never matched the fantasy. In fact, it was often a disastrous disappointment. The best nurseries struggled to meet the needs of very young children in a group setting. The worst were negligent, frightening and bleak: a nightmare of bewildered loneliness that was heartbreaking to watch. Children at this age – under three – want one thing only: the individual care of their own special person. Even the best-run nurseries cannot offer this. My professional sense of disquiet about the effects of this on children's wellbeing grew and grew, and so did that of many of my fellow psychologists. What is more, the evidence to match this disquiet began to accumulate in the research,[1, 2] until the need to publish this book could not be contained any further.

A changed world

The explosion in the use of group daycare for very young children has to be set in a wider context. The world has also changed in the last 30 years. As huge corporations spanned the earth and grew more powerful than governments, their influence over daily life grew too. People everywhere felt they had to work harder, even though they were more prosperous than ever before. There was enormous pressure to consume more material goods. Everything was getting faster, more stressed and money-oriented – the old values of caring and community interdependence were being swept away. People had less and less time for their marriages, their communities, their friends and even their own children. We weren't exactly slaves, we had a choice. But, to use Madeleine Bunting's phrase, we were 'willing slaves'[3] – somehow going along with this deteriorating quality of life without question.

The use of nursery care for very young babies was part of this trend. As a psychologist, and as a parent of children who would have to live in this new world, I feared where it was all leading: that millions of children would have inferior-quality childhoods, and that the most important attribute that makes us human – the ability to love and care for each other – was not being passed on as it should. It is a fundamental tenet of psychology that in the first three years of life we learn the most important lesson of our whole lifetime – how to love. By giving away this precious window of intimate time, I feared we were raising a colder, sadder, more stressed and aggressive generation of children who might forever struggle to know what closeness and inner peace really felt like.

This book presents much objective evidence, but it also carries a strong professional opinion for which I don't apologize. It is likely that some people will feel angry after reading it, and it may be unsettling for those who feel trapped by economic circumstances into placing their babies and toddlers in day nurseries when they would rather not. But my responsibility as a psychologist and educator is to be honest and to convey current findings and knowledge without gloss or deception.

So many voices in the parenting advice industry have a product to sell or an ideological agenda to advance. So few people are speaking on behalf of the children themselves. When I read childcare magazines and trendy books about parenting, their advice that 'whatever you choose is right for you' and 'your child will be happy if you are happy' sounds like feel-good rubbish – clever, slippery words that smooth over real concerns, and allay feelings of guilt that really should be listened to.

This is a parenting book that has a political message too. Successive UK governments have done a dismal job of supporting parents: leave provisions, job security and work flexibility laws are still decades behind progressive countries such as Denmark, Norway, France and especially Sweden (where there are today almost no babies attending daycare).[4] There are some signs of willingness in the current government to look more closely at the needs of young families. This book adds to the arguments for giving parents what they need to raise healthy and well-loved kids.

At first, I was afraid to release this book. Five years ago when I began writing, its message seemed so confronting, so against the tide. So I discussed it with hundreds of people – nursery directors and staff, psychologists, psychiatrists, parents, grandparents, academics, researchers. All of them gave me the same feedback – that 'someone had to speak up', that the message was 'urgently needed and long overdue'.

Helping you decide

It's likely you have come to this book with a specific aim: to try and decide whether your baby or toddler should spend time in a nursery or daycare centre. In the chapters that follow I will clearly lay out for you the best current information about just this. I will also explore what choices other parents are making and why. Stories of nursery care, and stories of real life families working out what to do will help you clarify your own priorities.

There has been much soul-searching about whether nursery care is a good idea, and also much widely-conflicting information. The 'daycare debate' has received more media coverage, and more concerted research by child development experts, than any other aspect of childrearing in the last 30 years. For a while the results were uncertain, but recently this situation has changed. New results from wide ranging and very large-scale studies have emerged that clarify the dangers, and explain why nursery care is far from what we might want for our children.[5, 6] These results, and the dramatic story of how they were uncovered, make up the core of this book. Once and for all these findings can clear up the question that parents most want answers to: 'Will nursery care harm my child?'

The answer, as you might suspect, is 'yes', often it will. But not always – under certain conditions, and when children have reached the right age, nurseries or, better still, pre-school education can be a plus. I will detail for you what these conditions and ages are.

The results may be alarming to some, but seem perfectly obvious to others. Finally, we are waking up to the fact that something is amiss in the way we rear our children, and this includes our glib assumption that group care in nurseries is probably okay.

To further help you make your mind up, I will explain the latest understanding of how a baby's brain develops, wonderful new discoveries about how they learn to love and think, and feel calm and resilient in the world. You can then appreciate the part that a loving parent can play, and how hard it is for people who are not close to your child to provide this.

In the last ten years, researchers have learned that a baby's brain grows whole new structures in response to the love and affection, and caring firmness, given during its first two years of life.[7] If this kind of intense love is not given at the right time, these areas of the brain do not grow properly and, as a result, there are abilities a child may never acquire. This is perhaps the most vital message of this book – *children raised without sufficient loving care do not become fully the human beings they were meant to be.*

This is shocking news, and it has jolted governments around the world to consider giving more attention to the needs of young families. It confirms what most of us have always felt deep down – that loving, patient and supported time with young babies is not a luxury, but a vital nutrient that we must provide. My hope is that this knowledge will strengthen you to follow your heart, and not the dictates of advertisers, governments, employers or other social forces around you. By the end of this book you will be well equipped to make the best decisions for your baby or toddler, to know why you are making these decisions, and to feel a real peace and strength that you are doing what is right.

Raising Babies aims to provide you with the resources for your own reflection and deeper thought. It not only involves you becoming as informed as possible but also sharpening your own perceptions and, in the end, listening to your own heart. The aim is not to tell you what to do, but to awaken your own sense of what you really want out of your life. This may set you at odds with the direction of the society around you, but as history has shown, that can often be a good thing.

This book won't change anyone's mind who doesn't want to hear its message, but it will give strength to those parents whose hearts have been troubled, and who feel something is wrong; who want their family life to be gentler, more happy and more loving than what has become the norm. To these parents, let me say – your heart is right, and you can find a better way. All my good wishes go with you.

Steve Biddulph

In a nutshell

- My friend's experience alerts me to the fact that the child-care choice is often made under pressure, and many young parents do not realize just where their true feelings lie until they have to part with their child.
- Society has become more materialistic and has fatally neglected the place of caring, community and family needs in our lives.
- Governments have failed to protect families from corporate pressures and many people can no longer afford to care for their own children.
- Quality nursery care appropriate to very young children does not exist. It is a fantasy of the glossy magazines.
- If your heart has been uneasy about these things, it is probably right. You CAN find a better way.

Part One

The Truth about Nurseries

What are nurseries really like?

Are they good for children under three?

What are other parents choosing – and why?

What does the research say?

How can I make the best life choices that won't harm my child?

1

What nursery is like

Becoming a parent for the first time is an unbelievable feeling. It is an intensely happy time, and yet frightening too. Having this tiny baby in your home, in your arms, you feel terribly responsible and want to give your child the best care that you can. As it dawns on you how utterly dependent a human baby really is, you can easily feel overwhelmed by its needs and demands. Gradually, through the struggles, the sleep deprivation, the altered sense of time, the totally re-arranged priorities, you and your child find a rhythm, and you discover you really can do it. You begin to live a very different, subtler, deeper kind of life.

And then you are faced with the decision, like an impending grief – to return to work or stay at home? People are urging you in different directions, but what do *you* want to do? The first thing is to realize that you really do have a choice. You may be surprised to learn what other people choose. Despite all the financial pressures, and the general feeling that both parents should be in the workforce, from government and employers, over 40 per cent of all UK parents choose that one of them will stay home until their children are of school age. (And these are surprisingly often people who choose to make financial sacrifices, and are not especially well off. Wealthier people have a long tradition of farming out their childcare, which continues to this day.) Of the rest, most 'primary caregivers' (by which researchers usually mean mothers) return gradually to part-time work, usually only after their child reaches two or three, and perhaps full-time work as their children get older and better able to cope with out-of-home care. (In around 5 per cent of families, the father stays at home, and the mother returns to full-time work at some time during the first five years.) And finally, it might surprise you to learn that only about 1 in 20 families put their baby straight into full-time, ten-hours-a-day nursery care before the baby is one year old. We will look at these choices and their pros and cons later in the book. For now the main point is – you *do* have a choice.

To choose wisely you must be informed; so the most important thing you must do, before committing yourself to any long-term plans, is go and find out what a nursery is really like. Forget the brochures, the glowing propaganda, and the cheery reassurances of those who want to persuade themselves that all is fine. For a decision this big you have to see for yourself. Not just a flying visit, or the official guided tour – 'look at the little toilets, aren't they cute?' – but an hour or more of melting into the background, quietly observing what goes on. It is a good idea to go alone the first time (without your baby), then you can ask to go back with your partner for a second look at a different time on a different day. The aim is to get an accurate sense of what it might be like to be a child spending ten hours a day in such a place.

Trusting your senses

As you enter the nursery's doors, the feeling and mood of the place will be immediately obvious. In fact it is something of a sensory overload. Here are some of the impressions you might form.

1 The lack of peace

There is something exhausting and overwhelming about so many small people in one confined space. It is noisy, even when the sounds are all happy, but add a certain amount of crying or angry shouts, and it is a stressful sound, which – apart from at 'nap time' (and that is rarely silent) – continues all day long.

Apart from the noise, there is a difficulty in keeping mental focus. Children at this age are capable of concentrated quiet play – imaginary games, chatting to themselves, being peaceful. But in this environment, it is not easy for them to settle: they run about, fight over toys, compete for adult attention. Carers share themselves as best they can, prevent fights, try to engage quiet or shy children, stimulate play activities, but there is often a feeling of jumble and coping, rather than enjoyment and peaceful concentration.

2 The sense of vulnerability

Childhood is an aggressive time – even at home, little children often resort to hitting, pulling, shouting, as they lack the skills to sort out conflict in better ways. But in a large group setting it gets worse. Groups of bigger boys, or meaner girls who physically or emotionally dominate things, can be a problem if your child is quieter or less assertive. Alternatively your child may become one of the dominators or bullies, as another way of dealing with the stressful environment. Under-twos are too young to nurture or befriend each other for more than a few seconds, or even play together co-operatively. Problems soon arise. A carer will usually intervene to protect the weaker children, but not always in time. It is only bumps and biffs and unkind words – they won't end up in hospital – but it is emotionally unsettling and scary to quite a few children. And there is no escaping it. Your child will be confined with the other children all together, all day long.

3 The lack of homeliness or a place of one's own

While there are interesting toys, play equipment and adults to encourage your child, there is no personal space; no quiet corner or toy or piece of furniture that is his or her own, apart from a coat hook and perhaps a piece of artwork taped on the wall. A child is rootless and unanchored, moving from one spot to another.

The baby room

'I went to a very nice, very expensive, highly-recom-mended nursery when I was nine months pregnant, in preparation for my return to work when my child was seven months old. I will never forget the feeling I got when I walked into the baby room. There were nine babies and three carers. One baby was being fed, one was having its nappy changed, and one other was being comforted as it was crying. The other six were sitting around in baby chairs in varying states of apathy and boredom. All I could think of was "these babies have been abandoned", and I wanted very strongly to cry.'

(website contributor, March 2006)

4 There are never enough adults to go around

Ratios of staff to children are always a compromise compared with what would be ideal. Usually there is one staff person to three or four babies, and one carer to eight to ten toddlers or older children. The staff do their best to share themselves around, but it is non-stop all day. A study commissioned by the Department of Education in 1999 found that the average amount of 1:1 attention per child was only eight minutes per day.[1] Staff respond to crises, divert problems, comfort a crying child, take someone to the toilet – and move on. Caring for so many children all day is difficult and draining – you will see the adults 'zone out' by taking mental breaks when they can, simply for self-preservation.

5 Some kids cope less well than others

You will notice some children having fun, showing mastery, and confidently talking to staff and claiming their attention. Others will hover on the edges, comfort themselves with repetitive movements, look warily about, or make forays into play and then retreat. They often seem detached, not quite there. They are far from happy, not showing any of the singing, laughing, chattering behaviour of the truly happy child. Yet to the staff these are 'good' children, not troublesome. They tend to be forgotten while more demanding kids take up the carers' time.

Hanging on the gate

I'm visiting a high-quality nursery on an observational visit. Today the weather is mild, and a group of three-year-olds have been taken outside to play. I notice that one girl is not playing with the others. She is hanging onto the gate into the yard, pulling at it in a listless repetitive action. I check my watch, and keep watching for about 20 minutes, and in that time she never stops the tugging action, rocking her body, gazing about as she does so. The young male carer is busy with other children, and seems oblivious to her. But now something happens: a boy, also a bit of a loner, is making his way along the fence line banging a stick on the railings. He stops when he reaches her – an obstacle in his path. They look at each other; I am too far away to tell if they speak. I'd like to report a human moment, a bit of contact, but sadly it's not to be. He solves the problem by making her not matter, he trails his stick across her middle, and continues on his way. She goes on pulling absently at the gate. The message of her body language seems so plain – 'Let me out of here.'

6 Some staff are more caring than others

You will notice that the staff members differ in personal qualities. Some are energetic, warm people, that you would love your child to be friends with. Some seem rather young to be caring for children. Some of the older ones look tense, exhausted, doing their best to be available but basically worn out. Still others seem bored, doing the bare minimum of 'work'. Of course, these things describe some parents too. But if this is your child, you have more reason and motivation to be at your best.

7 The staff care in a different way to a parent

The interactions with children – the way staff talk, hold them, respond to their emotions – is always affected by the fact that this is a professional relationship. There is a necessary coolness to everything. Eye contact is not the same. There is no time for long, peaceful, intimate moments. Concern has to be tempered, empathy withheld, because another ten or 20 children are there right now, ready to make their claim. In fact, staff would be in trouble – and we would be concerned – if they showed real affection and attachment to any particular child. What nursery staff offer is care, but it isn't love, and the difference is vast.

8 There is a mechanical, institutional quality to the day's events

Toileting, meals, nap time, nappy changing, face and hand washing, moving from activity to activity, are all mass activities. It's a rare staff member who sings to a baby or blows a raspberry on its tummy while changing its nappy – something a mother or father does all the time. This is institutional life. (One nursery made a video of the children's day, with a stationary camera, and then played it fast-forward at their annual parents' meeting as a joke. There were one or two laughs at the start, then everyone went very quiet. It all looked so regimented, so impersonal.)

A place to call home

Remember your childhood days – if you were lucky, you will recall the haven of your bedroom or living room, a favourite chair or corner, well-loved toys and books. You might remember hours spent in a smallish back garden, which seemed to you quite big, and had interesting, even scary, corners and hidey-holes, insects and birds, some stuff to climb on. And over it all, with any luck, a feeling of peace, safety, time, your own space to be absorbed in fantasy play and imagining, which in turn was stimulated by books read to you, stories and TV programmes you were allowed to watch. You had friends who visited with their parents, or came in from next door, and you played with them, mostly in groups of two or three. You developed fantasy games, which lasted for hours, and from which you had to be dragged away for supper or bedtime. Perhaps you had these things, but even if not, you probably wished you had, and you want your children to have them too. Childhood needs its time, and its space.

9 The presence of babies seems wrong

The younger the child, the less appropriate the environment of nursery care seems to be for their needs. In terms of the enjoyment, opportunities, interactions, it will be clear as you watch that older children are better suited to nursery than the younger ones. Playing in groups, being able to fend for themselves or lose themselves in activities such as painting or sand-play – all seem to be happening for the three- and four-year-olds, while the babies and toddlers seem lost, disengaged, given a peremptory cuddle or a short-lived bit of focus from a carer. They manage to get through the day, but it is not exactly happy. Older children enjoy nursery, younger ones tolerate it.

10 A day is a really long time

The final thing to notice on this visit to the nursery is how slowly time passes. You don't wonder at the high staff turnover, or the fact that many carers move on to more interesting or varied lines of work. But remember how time passes for a child. A day is a really long time when you are only two, even for a happy child. A day at home can be long too, but it is punctuated by being part of the parent's life – going about, meeting friends, shopping – in a way that can be made enriching and interesting. There is more variety and change in a child's world outside than inside the fences or walls of a daycare centre.

. . .

In the chapters that follow, you will find that each of these concerns, these 'seat-of-the-pants' observations, are shown by research to be factors that make a nursery a second-rate environment for children under three. You will also discover how hard it is to cater for this age range in a group setting, whereas for the over-threes it becomes the very thing that, in moderation, supplements what parents provide, and prepares children for school. The research picture supports what common sense might tell us, that distorting the natural social environment of children has disturbing results. However, you should trust your own impressions above all, as ultimately you have to decide for yourself if the research supports or denies your own common sense.

What nursery staff think of nurseries

The media loves telling horror stories of nurseries from hell, psycho-nannies or carers going off the rails, because these play to parents' greatest fears. In this book, we are more concerned with the most typical and likely experiences – what you can expect to find, rather than the extreme failures. One way to form an overall picture is to listen to the views of people who work in nurseries, and who have been thinking about this topic all their working lives.

In 2004, the BBC screened a documentary called *Nurseries Undercover*. Parents around the country watched in dismay as hidden cameras showed children being mistreated by staff and the dismal conditions in some nurseries. There was a spate of letters to newspapers around the country, including this one from Fiona Steele, a nursery director in London:[2]

'I have worked in too many nurseries, for too many years, to be surprised by the neglect, incompetence and casual cruelty the programme revealed. But I did feel angry.

'Everyone who talks about childcare, it seems, has a political agenda. But I am speaking purely from six years' personal experience of working in nurseries. And I can tell you there is indeed a problem with the quality of childcare in this country – however uncomfortable the truth is, however much we might want to avoid anything that appears to curb our freedom to be child-free parents.

'Parents send their children to nurseries for many differ-ent reasons: they might be single parents; they cannot afford not to work; they find parenting boring, or bonding difficult; they might have been persuaded that it will benefit their children's social development (when did this fallacy become accepted wisdom?); or they simply don't want to lose their place on the career ladder. Whatever the case, childcare is here to stay.

'Many children have been in my care since they were three months old. Part-time places are not cost-effective, so many are with us from 8 am to 6 pm, five days a week, and so spend the majority of their waking time with me and my colleagues.

'It is unthinkable that any child in our nursery would not receive immediate comfort and reassurance if they needed it (as was sadly the case in the documentary), but I am aware that many nurseries never engage emotionally with their children, maintaining a professional detach-ment. One nursery manager I know instructs her staff not to hug crying children because "it will make them soft".

'Nurseries have become big business. Large corporate structures are proliferating, with groups of nurseries being run from remote head offices where profit-driven, sales-oriented teams allow individual managers little say in the running of their nurseries.

'One (ex-retail) director of such a chain revealed that his ambition was to create a strong "brand", so that if you walked into any one, you would instantly know it was his. Everything would be the same: identical decor, identical staff uniforms, standard-issue toys. What has this to do with the care of children? It is not good practice, and yet it is awarded stars for excellence. Nursery owners, OFSTED inspectors and parents are obsessed with appearances, and the essence of good childcare is being lost.

'It has been one of the saddest aspects of my career that not once – not at college or on any training course – has anyone ever mentioned the primary importance of emotional security and happiness in the development of a small child. Many staff (and parents) are insufficiently informed to understand that many demands we make of small children are unrealistic.'

Perhaps this is just one person's minority view? It appears not – similar comments came from no less a person than Rosemary Murphy, the head of the National Day Nursery Association, which represents more than 3,000 private nurseries. Rosemary told the *Guardian* newspaper:

'I am concerned that Britain is stumbling into changes about how small children are cared for without anything like the kind of informed public debate necessary. There's a woeful lack of public debate. We need to look at this whole question very carefully for two reasons: firstly, because it is fundamental to get child development right, and secondly, because we need to think about what child-care should look like: are we developing the right kind of system?'[3]

Coming from someone who represents the industry, these frank comments have to be a source of real concern.

In a nutshell

- Visit a day nursery: your own senses will tell you that it is a difficult and less than ideal place for an under-three-year-old child. It lacks the kind of focus or empathy that is needed for a young child to feel loved, or grow and learn well.
- A nursery director says that coldness and uncaring behaviour is widespread across Britain's nurseries. The industry's spokesperson herself is deeply concerned about where nurseries are going.

2

Slammers and sliders

Childhood today is nothing like it was for preceding generations, especially for very young children. In 1981, only 24 per cent of mothers returned to work before their baby was one year old. Today the figure is over 60 per cent. (Of course, 95 per cent of fathers return to work too.) As a result, almost a quarter of a million UK children under three attend a day nursery full- or part-time.

Worldwide, the number of babies and toddlers spending all day in nursery care has *quadrupled* in just ten years. Daycare was originally intended for three- and four-year-olds, but its use has spread downwards; sometimes babies are now put into nurseries and crèches when they are just days old. The hours have got longer too: millions of children under three are in daycare centres *ten hours a day, five days a week* in America, Australia, Brazil, Japan and other industrialized countries across the globe.

This large-scale group care of the very young is a recent thing. It has happened without prior research or understanding (compared with, for instance, the invention of kindergarten, which was specifically designed with child development needs in mind). If it turns out that early child-care is a damaging thing, then millions of lives will have been adversely affected. As we will see later, the chemistry of these children's bodies and even the structure of their brains may well turn out to be different – but not in good ways.

Two kinds of nursery user

In the past it was hard to find accurate statistics about the extent of daycare. Statistics for children under three often did not specify how early it began, and for how many hours a week. Finally, in the late 1990s, some of the statistics were 'disaggregated' – that is, broken down to see if there are different types of choices hidden away in the 'average' figures. A remarkable discovery was made – *there are two distinct patterns of nursery care usage* that indicate two different sets of parenting beliefs and values.[1] In private, childcare researchers have come to call these two groups 'slammers' and 'sliders'.

Slammers are parents who 'slam' their child into nursery care as early in life as possible, and for as many hours a day as they are permitted. This can be from as early as 7 am until 6 pm or even later, usually for the full working week. These parents are essentially only with their babies at night-time and weekends. This group has begun to be studied extensively, and they have proven to be very consistent. Slammers usually place their babies in a nursery well before they are six months of age, and once there, tend to keep them there, full-time, until the child starts school. That means their children spend over 12,000 hours in a nursery before their fifth birthday. (This is more hours than they will spend in the schoolroom in the following 12 years – an astonishing amount of time.) While slammers might deny it, the choices they make essentially say: 'This child does not come first in my life – it fits around my life. My career/income/social life/education are the defining factors of my time and energy.' Slammers are only a small group – *less than 5 per cent of parents*. That is a small percentage, but it's still a lot of children – approximately 100,000 out of the UK's 2 million under-threes, and the number is growing, especially among urban professionals. It is a lifestyle that is often represented in magazines, and by corporate propaganda, as the ideal and desirable lifestyle, influencing others to see this as the norm.

Morning delivery

It is just after 7 am, and I am taking an early morning run in a town I am visiting for a few days. Turning down a leafy side street to get away from the noise and smell of traffic, I come across a rather posh nursery behind a big fence. A sign announces that it offers 'early learning opportunities' for children from birth to five. I pause for breath and study the sign, noticing the hours – 7 am to 7 pm each day. Suddenly I am startled by the sound of tyres skidding on gravel. A large four-wheel drive vehicle mounts the kerb just feet from where I am standing, so close that it makes me jump backwards. It comes to an abrupt stop, rocking on its springs. A frowning, smartly-dressed man leaps out, slams his door, strides around the car and pulls out a bundle from the back seat, from which I can just glimpse a tiny baby's face peering out. The man barrels through the childproof gate and into the centre. In less than a minute he is out again and the car screeches away. The whole thing is like a cash drop at a bank. Maybe he is having a really bad day. I hope that's what it is, and not just another morning. In either case though, I would hate to be that baby.

Sliders, by contrast, are parents who only place their children into nursery care gradually, and often much later – perhaps not until they are aged two or more – and usually for much shorter periods of time each week. This is closer to what child development theory would advise. (For more detail of what is appropriate by age and gender of child; see the Appendix at the end of this book.) Slider parents use nursery care cautiously, sometimes reluctantly, but balanced against a wish to get back some of the financial independence and self-esteem that goes with being in the paid workforce. They use nursery more when their child is over three and ready for some social and educational input. Sliders consider their children's needs and attempt to find a family-friendly balance. Significantly, and thankfully, sliders are a much larger group – they outnumber slammers by about 8:1.

Of course, parents sometimes have to slide faster than they would wish. They are often forced to do so by economic pressures, as well as the loneliness that confronts mothers in commuter suburbs or apartment blocks where there is little other way of participating in the wider world. Since fathers are assumed to be going to work, the problems – and joys – of parenthood are largely left with the mother, though in a significant positive trend, increasing numbers of couples now reverse roles, or even take a year off work in rotation, so that their children can have a loving parent to care for them for at least the first two years of life. This non-sexist arrangement seems to work quite well, but again requires employer flexibility and some willingness by fathers to break old stereotypes.

The health consequences of distant parenting

Does it really matter if a child is close to its parents? We usually assume that close parent–child bonds are the fundamentals of a happy start to life. But why must this be so? Do we really need closeness to grow up well?

A unique and little-known American study was carried out into just this question, beginning with young adults in the 1950s and revisiting them 35 years later when they were in late middle age. Detailed interviews and medical assessments were carried out at the start of the study, including questions about how close they felt to their mother and their father.[2]

When the subjects were tracked down 35 years later, their medical records were accessed and extensive assessments and interviews were carried out. What was discovered was quite astounding: *91 per cent of those who did not have a close relationship with their mothers (by their own assessment) had been diagnosed with a serious medical illness in mid-life – double the rate of those who reported a warm relationship.* Closeness to fathers, or the lack of it, predicted similar differences in health. Worst off of all in health were those who had been close to neither mother or father.

The health conditions included heart disease, cancer, ulcers, alcoholism, hypertension and chronic asthma. As recent brain and immune system studies have revealed, love keeps you well. And the effects of love in childhood seem to keep on maintaining your health through life. Researcher Dr Norman Anderson, who reviewed these studies in 2003, was able to find over 20 similar studies, with 55,000 participants in total, all of which validated these findings. Being close to one's parents does matter, and it matters long after you have grown up.

Home-raised children

Apart from slammers and sliders, there is still a large group of parents – around 60 per cent – whose children never see the inside of a day nursery, and who move from family home, spiced up with time in the care of grandparents, relatives, friends or childminders, directly to pre-school and full-time school. It is interesting to compare countries in this regard. In

Germany and Italy this home-rearing group is large – about 90 per cent, in Sweden around 50 per cent, but in the US only 35 per cent. The variations between countries indicate different values in those cultures but, even allowing for these differences, in every developed country a significant number of parents – usually mothers, but increasingly also fathers – forego employment opportunities, interrupt their personal goals, and direct their energies towards home, children and community, at least for this short period of their lives, and would not have it any other way. When interviewed, these parents invariably say they would like their role recognized and valued more, and would also like their eventual return to work to be made easier by flexible work and retraining support. They also argue strongly for paid parental leave, so that the valuable service they provide in parenting is rewarded by the larger community.

These three lifestyles – slamming, sliding, or home-rearing – are the options parents of the under-threes can choose between. You too have these choices – or should do. Many of us in the 1960s and 1970s fought hard to win the right for women to have careers, and this fight still continues. But increasingly now we have to fight for the right of parents – of both sexes – *to step out of paid careers* if they choose, in order to properly care for their children; and this will certainly be demanded by future generations. We have a right to parent, and children have a right to receive full-time love.

Nursery uptake and social class

It is interesting to note that attitudes to nursery care are different in different social groups across the UK. The Sure Start programme – the government's system of parent support centres and home visitors – has been acclaimed worldwide for providing help at the most beneficial and crucial time. Sure Start includes a range of services, among them the offering of childcare nursery places. Yet in the traditional blue-collar regions of the UK, organizers often find it almost impossible to get parents to take up the nursery places available. A centre director told the *Guardian* newspaper:

'Parents round here don't want to use day nurseries – they don't want to leave their children with people they don't know. This is their precious child and they don't want to hand them over to strangers. We're registered and inspected by OFSTED and we have qualifications, but they don't trust all that. We're attempting a big cultural shift.'[3]

The article went on to report that:

'On the other side of Birmingham, on another large housing estate, Chelmsley Wood, the mothers at the Sure Start project have very strong views on the subject. As one of the first projects of its kind, it runs the services parents asked for – a drop-in centre, programmes to support parents, encouraging them to read and sing nursery

rhymes with their children – but it has no daycare. One of
the mothers, Kate, is planning to go back to work, but
only when her son is at school: "Tom is my only child, he's
so precious. I'm frightened and not sure about daycare. It
would worry me too much, that he was spending too much
time with other people."'

Another mother, Clare, went back to work after three months
with her first child. That was eight years ago, and this time
around she's determined to do it differently: 'I missed out on
so much and I said I would never do that again. I will wait
until my children are in full-time school.'

Blue-collar parents are much more reluctant to use nurseries than the middle classes. So are immigrant parents and
refugees. A higher value is placed on family cohesion among
the poor, and often it is all that stands between them and
annihilation. Many US daycare centres now deliberately
recruit staff from Hispanic backgrounds because these young
women tend to be more loving, tender, patient and good
humoured – more natural, and good with children. Parents
prefer them. White carers tended to be more self-centred, less
caring and colder. Are those cultures that are closer to an
agrarian, family-oriented way of life the last receptacles of the
ability to love children? What does that say for where we are
heading?

Having it all?

The media must accept a lot of the responsibility for shaping the attitudes and beliefs of young parents as to what is normal: 'You can have it all' is a very advertiser-friendly editorial line. A recent magazine article on childcare choices featured photos of unusually good-looking mothers with their babies at the beach. One of the women – a fashion model – told the interviewer: 'I stayed home for the first six months. Then I put him in a nursery full-time and returned to work. I really needed my independence.' It was a strange choice of words – a mother is not dependent on her child. (Independence is what you get when you leave your parents – not when you leave your child!) Perhaps what she really meant was 'I really needed my *freedom*.' To be free of this demanding little person, to focus on *me* again. Except, put that way, it doesn't sound quite so edifying.

Several years ago one of the largest bookstore chains in the UK asked me to write a book on 'Choosing Childcare – deciding what is right for you'. I was excited about this idea since it was a chance to put across some of the concerns you have been reading about here. I wrote back to them just to be sure. Were they aware that I believed most alternatives to parental care of babies to be seriously second-rate? That I would not recommend nursery care or nannies for children under the age of two? No, it turned out they had not read any of my books, though they had sold millions of them! You could hear the back-pedalling all the way from Australia. They wanted to sell books that made people feel good whatever they chose, and perhaps I wasn't their man. So, with courtesy and warmth, we parted ways! I guess they found somebody else.

What do you *prefer*?

Dr Catherine Hakim, a researcher at the London School of Economics, has attracted worldwide attention for some new thinking about the whole question of mothers and paid work.[4] Hakim came to the enlightened realization that all of the statistics about childcare that one ever reads were based on what people were *doing*. But what if they instead asked people what they would *prefer* to do? Asking this question revealed a completely different picture. Up until that point, governments had made a sweeping assumption – all mothers (and fathers) want to work, and like doing so. In a way, this was as stereotyped as the 1950s idea that all mothers liked staying at home and cooking scones. When people were interviewed about their actual preferences, Hakim found three distinct groups:

1. *Home-centred women* who give priority to children and family life, and prefer not to do paid work at all. This group makes up about 20 per cent of women in the UK. (And probably of men too, if they were given the choice.)
2. *Work-centred women* who give priority to careers. Again, this group makes up about 20 per cent.

3. *Adaptive women* who combine work and family life, but saw work as being something to fit around their family life, rather than the reverse. This group makes up about 60 per cent.

(The focus solely on work and family can be limiting here: most women are also involved in activism, education, and other pursuits that define their lives more broadly than these two specific roles. SB)

Hakim argued that by basing policies on the work-centred 20 per cent, just because they conformed to certain feminist expectations, the home-centred group were disadvantaged, as were the adaptive women, who often preferred shorter hours and other reforms that made it possible to meet the needs of children. This argument had huge implications for governments – for instance, the funds and tax breaks poured into subsidizing nursery care might be better spent on subsidizing those parents who wanted shorter working hours, or simply wish to stay at home and care for their children – and could do so more cheaply and better than nurseries could manage.

Hakim's work has strong statistical support, and has galvanized discussion, since it allows for more diversity of choice, and is patently more realistic. It also brought to the fore some of the real tensions current in our lives. For instance, at one time it was male managers who did not understand the needs of women in the workforce. Staff I worked with recently at a large university told me a sad story of how the women on the academic staff had eagerly awaited a woman vice-chancellor, who would understand their needs for maternity leave, leave to care for sick children and flexible work hours, only to find that the woman who got the job was far more judgemental and less compassionate than her male predecessor. Their situation went into reverse, and 20 years of gradual gains were wiped out in a year.

Many magazines and press articles have described the 'Mummy Wars', in which fierce divisions exist between stay-at-home mothers and mothers in the paid workforce. It's likely that both groups secretly envy some of the options enjoyed by the other. Hakim's research would suggest that a large proportion of us would like the benefits of a timely return to work, but not at the expense of our children. It doesn't seem too hard for employers and governments to meet this reasonable demand. If we also add an availability of fathers to do their part in the early years, then the problem is not insurmountable.

For a young couple contemplating starting a family, or with a new baby at home, it is important to do some hard thinking. We human beings are easily confused, and very much herd creatures. We do what everyone else does. We accept platitudes that really don't make sense, but sound good. We are told 'what's good for you is good for them'. Also our own background has a big effect. If we don't have a strong experience of parental love in our own childhood, we might not know what we are losing.

There is intense and intelligent discussion going on in the UK today about these choices. Parents in the past have often been fobbed off with bland reassurance, as if parenthood somehow softens the brain, but we are now more educated, more questioning and more networked than ever. And, fortunately, the answers are now emerging to address our concerns. In the following chapters, we will look at this in depth. The big question in choosing between slamming, sliding or staying at home, is: what is best *from a child's point of view*?

A woman who asks tough questions

The scene is a large national conference of women lawyers in Sydney, Australia, and the topic is a popular one – combining parenthood with a career. The speakers are all of one mind: 'There is still much work to be done to overcome discrimination. It is tough being a professional woman and a mother as well.' The convenor, thanking the morning's speakers, adds her own exhortation: 'Don't let anyone tell you that you shouldn't be working.'

Then, unexpectedly, a hand goes up in the audience. Heads turned to watch as a tall, bespectacled young woman is handed a microphone. 'No one has ever told me *not* to work,' she says, in a clear and thoughtful voice. 'These days all the pressure we get is to work full-time and to have a successful career.' She pauses to allow this to sink in. 'What no one talks about is taking time out to care for our children. That's the message young women never hear today.' You could hear a pin drop.

The woman's name is Cathleen Sherry. She is, in her mid-thirties, already a tenured lecturer in law. Sherry is unusual in her profession, because with a family of three young children, she has reduced her workload by two-thirds, including taking several years off work completely. In Australia, she is a voice of the generational shift within feminism. Since that moment at the conference, she has featured in many media stories, and has written a series of articles of her own. She is saying, loud and clear: 'What about the children?'

Sherry had come through a conversion experience of her own. When preparing to start her family, she sought out older women lawyers whom she knew were combining family and full-time work. She assumed that she could find role models and mentors to show her how it was done. Instead, she got a huge shock. When these women opened up to her, their lives sounded like a nightmare. They told stories of putting weeks-old babies into daycare, battling exhaustion, failing to acquire mothering skills, having problems with breastfeeding, feeling miserable and conflicted. Some of the older women told her of destroyed marriages and adolescent children with serious problems. A few of her informants did their best to put a positive spin on it all, but others were frankly shattered. As Sherry said, 'There was no one that I spoke with who gave me the feeling – this is how I would want my life to be.' The blueprint she was looking for – happily combining family and full-time work – did not exist, at least not in the world of the law.

There was more. As a rights lawyer, often advocating for children in the courtroom, Sherry saw a contradiction. That the sacred cow of the 1990s, a woman's right to do what she wanted, was a logical fallacy. The needs of every person in the family and community had to be considered together, and balanced against each other. She told one interviewer:

'No one has an absolute right to a career – men or women. If you choose to have children, your major responsibility is to care for them properly, and if that affects your career, it affects your career. But no one wants to acknowledge this reality ... There is more than a dollop of hypocrisy in the fact that men who spend excessive hours in the workplace and little time with their children are considered substandard parents and yet women who do the same are considered "supermums".'

Sherry is tough on men too.

'Childcare allows men to avoid responsibility for their children. Women have to pay for others to look after their children because men aren't willing to cut back on their work hours to do their share of the parenting. If women go back to work, it should be men, not children, who alter their lives accordingly.'

Cathleen Sherry is a nuanced kind of feminist who thinks children have rights too, and she knows that there is more to life than what money can buy. She is also a strong believer in governments providing proper support to those vulnerable women – especially single mothers – who need financial support to care for their children properly. She does not see it as just that poorer women should be forced into the workforce, to the cost of their children's nurture. As she points out, in most countries the law only requires a child care centre to have one carer for every five babies.

'It is like having a mother on her own caring for quintuplets. One baby wakes and needs to be fed. Another is crying, needing comfort but has to wait; they all have to wait their turn for comfort, affection, cuddles, – all the things that babies need ... In maternity hospitals, it is no longer the done thing to have newborn babies lined up in a nursery with a couple of nurses looking after them. That is seen as terrible. Mothers are strongly persuaded to have their babies with them 24 hours a day. Yet six weeks later is okay to put ten of them in a nursery with just two carers. It doesn't make sense.'

In a nutshell

- The statistics about nursery-care usage are deceiving unless analysed properly.
- Slammers – who put their babies straight into full-time daycare – make up less than 5 per cent of the UK's parents.
- Sliders – who gradually use some care, often not starting until three years of age and often part-time – make up about 35 per cent.
- Those who use no group care at all, only themselves supplemented by grandparents and friends occasionally, make up around 60 per cent. Prominent in this sector are blue-collar parents and ethnic minorities.
- Catherine Hakim believes government policies should meet the needs of adaptive and stay-at-home parents, while at present they only serve the work-driven 20 per cent. She's right.
- The big question is – what is best for the child?

3

Does nursery harm under-threes?

The daycare debate first began to really heat up about thirty years ago. As the use of day nurseries for very young children increased in the 1970s, child development experts began to be concerned about what this kind of care might do to the child. The effects of separation from parents in wartime had become a major area of study, and was already leading to changes in how children were treated – for instance, it was realized that children in hospitals needed to have their parents visit daily or, even better, stay with them, while in the past they had been actively prevented from visiting more than once a week. Dr John Bowlby's research into 'attachment' problems in children separated from their parents was now cited to suggest that the bond between mother and child, known to be necessary to the healthy development of children, was endangered if a mother entered full-time work too soon, and that children in nurseries would not develop well without the secure and loving input that a parent or family member provides.[1]

Vested interests

At the same time, a new industry – and a new profession – was mushrooming around the demand for well-conducted nurseries, and 'Early Childhood' departments sprang up in universities and technical colleges, aimed at training child-care directors and teachers. These departments were well funded by governments on both the left and right, who saw the tax advantages of having everyone in the workforce, with the additional advantage of appearing progressive and woman-friendly at the same time.

These departments were often set up in universities that already had psychology departments with child development units within them, which trained psychologists and child welfare workers. These parallel faculties often found themselves preaching opposite points of view – though both were committed to the well-being of children, they had different ways of arriving there. A common statement from the Early Childhood school of thought was the fatalistic one that nursery care 'was here to stay' and that therefore 'we have to do what we can to make it as good as possible'. The opposing camp felt that parents must be alerted to the drawbacks of nursery care and influenced not to abandon their children in the rush towards self-obsession that gave them the label of the 'Me generation'. Clearly, there was some truth on both sides, but the emotive and politicized situation did not make for objective research.

In the early 1980s there was continuing disquiet about infant daycare, but little evidence of harm was reported in studies at that time. The worries were theoretical and, to some degree, based on intuition or folk wisdom about what children need. Yet it made sense to be cautious – half a million years of childrearing was being tampered with, and we didn't really know the long-term effects. The two sides of the debate became quite passionate: people on both sides wrote angry letters to the newspapers, grandmothers argued with their daughters about putting their precious grandchildren into a nursery. More than a few offered to mind the children instead.

Early concerns

Then, in the late 1980s, a number of studies began to report early concerns.[2] Children who were studied at ages three to eight and who had spent long hours in nursery care from a young age were found by researchers to more often have 'elevated levels of aggression and non-compliance' – in plain language, they were hitting other children and adults, and not doing what they were told. A second kind of damage was also reported – a weakening of attachment between parent and child, especially in those parents who did not have a good bond with their child in the first place. The studies were repeated and made more rigorous, since the findings were not popular or appreciated by many in the field. When the results came in – by now it was the early 1990s – a trio of risk factors emerged which *when combined together*, indicated a stronger risk of harm.[3] These were:

1. Starting nursery care very young;
2. Attending for long hours each week (20 hours or more);
3. Being in this form of care over many years of childhood.

In short, *too early, too much, and for too long.*

Some researchers disputed these findings and raised valid questions about other factors which might be causing the damage.[4] For instance, was it just that some care was not of good quality? This was a favoured explanation (in spite of the fact that most of the centres studied were high-quality university centres convenient for the researchers). Another was that poor parenting was the real reason for these children's problems. Yet another was that children of low-income families were more often the ones in care and so were more damaged anyway.

It was even argued that these children were not being aggressive or defiant, or poorly bonded, so much as assertive, confident and independent, and that this was a plus. Being in group settings for much of their childhood had given these children the ability or need to stand up for themselves and get what they wanted. And what could be wrong with that?

Over time, the experts in the field became more bitterly divided, objectivity suffered, and careers were made and broken. It all got very nasty, as disputes in academia tend to do. Research projects that did not meet the needs of the prevailing (pro-nursery care) ideology were suppressed or abandoned. I remember writing to a young woman researcher whose paper had been presented at a conference. It was a study showing that carers did not give the kind of attention or responsiveness to children that the parents did, when observed meticulously by researchers videotaping through a one-way mirror. The researcher sent a copy of her paper to me, but when I opened the envelope, scribbled across the front was a plea not to quote or publicize her findings. Apparently it was at odds with what her university – in fact the whole field at the time – wanted her to find out.

This division among experts was reflected in wider society. The infamous 'Mummy Wars' indicated a major philosophical clash of values that split the culture. 'Women had to be free' declared one side. 'But what about the children?' cried the other. Both sides called each other names.

Pretty soon parents themselves, as well as the experts, grew unhappy with the stereotyped divisions and began seeking a middle way. They also began to see that the fault sometimes lay in the wider system of a corporate society that was harming families and robbing people of real choice. Important social campaigns for flexible working hours, guaranteed return to work, retraining, and for adequate amounts of paid parental leave made slow but significant progress, so that there was less of an impossible choice for young parents between full-time work or full-time parenthood. More progressive countries such as Sweden and Germany bit the bullet and addressed these questions, giving more support at home and flexible conditions at work to help young parents whichever way they chose. Both of these countries allowed three years' parental leave (and for the first year, close to full pay) so that a parent could be assured their job would be there to return to. Those countries with less of a social democratic tradition, the UK and particularly the US (where people were much more at the mercy of big business and weak regulation), experienced sharper social divides and real hardship for low-income parents, who were simply forced to both work to survive. The concept of the 'living wage', allowing one wage earner to support a family, so hard fought for by trade unions early last century, had been destroyed.

In the US, and in much of the developing world, things were made worse by a widespread problem of low-quality, overcrowded and unregulated daycare provided for desperate blue-collar parents – a problem that has remained to this day. Even the most ardent advocates of nursery care have remained critical of the poor standard and unresourced nature of many centres. 'Quality care' became the pivotal argument and the heart of the campaign: 'If it is good quality, it will be all right.' In fact, the inference was that quality care was better than what you can give at home. This was the state of play by about 1995, and few dared to say otherwise. Yet this was about to come tumbling down.

At last, some answers

In the 1990s, because of the critical importance of the whole question, the confusion among parents, and the widespread disagreement amongst experts, a number of governments were persuaded that something had to be done. In the US, the UK and half a dozen other countries, very large long-term studies, bringing together teams of leading researchers, were set in motion to try and establish the truth once and for all. Was nursery care harmful? And if so, under what circumstances, and why?

The most comprehensive US study ever undertaken, by the National Institute of Child Health and Development (NICHD for short), involved over 1,000 children from ten diverse locations across the United States. Results have been released progressively since it began in 1991.[5, 6]

In the UK, the 'EPPE', or Effective Provision of Pre-School Education study, based at the University of London, followed the lives of 3,000 children from babyhood onwards – and concentrated especially on the three- to five-year age group – with extensive interviews and assessments of children's behaviour and academic performance. This study reported its results in 2004.[7]

Another large-scale study of 1,200 children was designed and carried out by acclaimed childcare expert Penelope Leach, together with academics Kathy Sylva and Alan Stein. This study revisited babies at 10, 18, 36 and 51 months of age and its results were announced in late 2005.[8]

None of the studies was purely objective – the US study team were predominantly academics who strongly supported daycare for philosophical reasons. Alison Clarke-Stewart, one of the US study authors, was a ferocious advocate, and dedicated a pro-daycare book to her son, 'who spent the first year of his life in daycare so I could work on this book'.[9] The UK's

EPPE study focused on the cognitive benefits of pre-school, and was funded by a government apparently committed to getting all mothers into the workforce. It was nonetheless a well-designed and balanced study, and this showed in the results. The Leach study was probably the most independent. Although Penelope Leach has long been one of the world's best advocates of children's needs, she is committed to doing this by also considering the needs of parents, and her recommendations are always eminently practical.

These three studies, along with others in countries ranging from Australia[10] to Norway, have produced a massive and highly significant amount of data which is still being analysed, and more is being generated as the children's lives continue to unfold. While not answering every question, these studies have overcome many of the problems of earlier research, and laid to rest many misconceptions. They have also lead to a considerable change of viewpoint among those who felt that nursery care was at worst harmless, and at best a positive thing for children under three years of age.

What the studies found

Across the three large studies, six specific questions were being asked.

1. Does the accumulated amount of time spent by babies, toddlers and young children in nursery care lead to emotional harm?

2. If so, does poor-*quality* nursery care provide the real explanation for this, or is extensive nursery care harmful, even if it is of good quality?

3. Might not the quality of *parenting* be the real reason for these problems in children who have been in nursery care for long periods from early in life? (In other words, do less able parents use nursery care more, so that these children have problems for that reason, and not from the care itself?)

4. Is there a cut-off point where nursery care becomes damaging? For instance, is ten hours a week – or 20, or 30 – a safer option than full-time care?

5. Does the timing of starting care have a bearing? For instance, what if you wait until a child is one year old before using nursery care? What if you use nursery care for six months, but then stop and keep your child at home? And so on. (For individual parents, these are important questions.)

6. And finally, if there is harm, does it heal over time or get worse? Under what conditions does either happen?

Here, in summary, is what was found across all three studies.

1 Yes, there is some damage

In the NICHD 2004 results,[11] only 6 per cent of children had noticeable behaviour problems in the under-ten-hours-a-week cohort, while almost three times as many – 17 per cent – did so in the over-30-hours-a-week group. According to the researchers' report, these problems included 'disobedience at school (being defiant, talking back to staff); getting into many fights; showing cruelty, bullying or meanness to others; physically attacking other people; and being explosive and showing unpredictable behaviour'. These increases were not large, but they were present in a large number of children.

The EPPE study likewise reported that 'high levels of group care before the age of three (and particularly before the age of two) were associated with higher levels of anti-social behaviour at age three'.

The Leach study reported nursery-cared-for babies and toddlers to have 'higher levels of aggression', and to be 'more inclined to become withdrawn, compliant and sad'. Dr Leach told a newspaper that 'the social and emotional development of children cared for by someone other than their mothers is definitely less good'. (The Leach study also compared different kinds of care outside nurseries, and found childminders and nannies, grandmothers and family and friends to be better than nurseries, though not as good as the child's own parents. These, of course, were general findings, and individual situations could be very different.) Dr Leach was at pains to point out that in the case of a depressed or unresponsive parent, or one with serious social problems, a carer would be a positive. It was the responsiveness that mattered.

For reasons described later in this book (see Chapter 4), discipline is only really successful if it comes from a person who loves the child, which may explain why behavioural problems are the main symptom displayed by children who have spent too much time in care.

2 The quality of care doesn't prevent the damage

Perhaps most significantly for the researchers and parents, the quality of care – how good, stable, caring and education- ally rich the settings were – had only a partial effect on the behaviour outcomes. Quality of care mattered a great deal, for reasons other than the ones being studied – it certainly had a bearing on cognitive (thinking) skills and literacy, compared with lower quality nurseries. Also children receiv- ing more one-to-one time in daycare centres with more and better trained staff were less stressed. But quality could not completely remove the damage done by 'too early, too much, too long'. The EPPE authors reported that 'while higher qual- ity of care could reduce the "antisocial/worried behaviour", it could not eliminate it', and the NICD authors concurred.

This finding had huge ramifications because it went against everything that had previously been believed. The mantra of the 1990s had been that poor outcomes were due to poor-quality nurseries. The new studies seemed to indicate that loving parents give something to children, that cannot be substituted for by paid staff. Quality care, while it was very important, was not the panacea that had been hoped for: it was still 'stranger care', and in a group rather than individual setting more normal to childhood needs, and this mattered to the proper development of secure and non-aggressive chil- dren.

3 Parenting quality matters most

There are some things that matter even more than the presence or absence of nursery care in a child's development. This is important to remember and every researcher is at pains to point it out. The most significant factor of all in determining child mental health was called by researchers 'maternal sensitivity'; the ability to respond warmly and sensitively (with enough fine tuning) to the needs of the child. This depends on the mother (or father) being sufficiently calm, supported and free from pressures to make the child their focus, and sufficiently resourced both materially and emotionally with friends and other outlets, so that they are not depressed, lonely or overwhelmed by the natural demands of parenthood. This quality relies on parents having the opportunity, through time and practice, to build a sensitive relationship – to get to know their baby and its nature, its needs, and its means of communicating these needs.

But even though parenting quality is more important than the amount of nursery care, they do affect each other. The studies found that one of the dangers to children was that 'too early, too much, too long' use of nursery care could weaken maternal sensitivity – or rather, prevent it from developing. This happened most often in mother–baby pairs where the relationship was already weak. In short, a mother who uses a lot of nursery care may get on less well with her baby because the time for their relationship to grow is not sufficient. An early dependence on daycare may prevent a parent and child from growing a responsive and strong relationship. Mother (or father) and baby may simply never have a chance to become close, and this could affect their relationship for a life-time.

4 Less is better, but there is no safe threshold

The negative effects of nursery care did not have a specific threshold or safety level in terms of the hours spent in care. The more nursery care a child receives, the greater the effects received, in a proportional amount. The researchers refer to this as a 'dose-related effect', and it is a strong pointer to a causal link. There isn't a safe level of nursery care usage for the under-threes (but at the same time, a little is better than a lot).

5 Timing is crucial

It turned out that timing was important, and that the 'sliders' were getting it right by waiting; in fact, it was essential to wait until *after the child was two* to avoid harmful effects. The NICHD study found that it did not make any difference whether parents placed their children into nursery care during the first or second year of their life – the damage effect remained the same. An 18-month-old was as vulnerable as a four-month-old in this regard.

For anyone who knows children, this stands up to the test of common sense. The toddler is an emotionally vulnerable being, acutely aware of its social environment, who loves it, and with whom it feels safe. A toddler fears strangers, and is strongly bonded to one or two trusted adults. A toddler is not yet able to play happily with other children, needs lots of adult attention, and also requires understanding and help with behaviour in order to learn self-control.

In fact, in some ways a baby under six months old is easier to be cared for by a non-family member – children are less fussy about who is cuddling them at this age, though the need for a loving and highly attentive and relaxed carer is still great. As will be discussed in Chapter 4 (on brain development), this is still the most important age to get it right.

6 The damage is moderate but widespread

Notwithstanding the above points, it is important to realize that the degree of harm caused by extensive use of childcare is moderate, at least as far as could be detected in this kind of study. However, what was found – and what the experimenters were at pains to point out – was that the effect was widespread. Dr Leach put it this way: 'a small but significant difference in a large group of children'.

Professor Jay Belsky, one of the NICHD authors, was to put significant weight on this when some commentators suggested that the damage was too small to matter. He observed that the effect was pervasive across all types of family and children – when all the compounding factors were removed using powerful statistical techniques, rich or poor, single or married parents, black, Hispanic or white, all were affected. This suggested that this small kernel of damage was enduring and real, and not easily erased.

He pointed out the social problems that occur when large numbers of children are affected even in a small way and expressed concern for schools, as large numbers of children with even moderate behaviour problems begin to overload teachers and systems – a problem that is now being widely reported around the world. Such children might worsen each other's social environment. A classroom with two or three problem behaviour children can be managed, but with eight or ten this can become unmanageable.

As we know from research into the harm caused by tobacco and other large-scale environmental health problems, establishing harm is quite a hard thing to do. The measuring tools in these daycare studies are relatively weak and are based on observation and interview – we do not really know what is happening inside these children, nor do we know how these changes will interact, for instance, with later stresses, with school challenges, or in ways that do not emerge until they are adults. The negative effects found in these studies may not be the only ones that have occurred and the most important kinds of damage may not show up for some time. (As I will argue in the second part of this book, what happens inside babies' brains is so delicate and important, that its likely these studies barely touch the surface of what is missed out on in group stranger care.)

Cognitive learning

Not all the effects of daycare are negative. The EPPE study largely focused on the three- to five-year age group, and it found that *for this age group*, pre-school experience boosted cognitive learning (thinking and reasoning skills), especially for at-risk or impoverished children. It noted, though, that the benefits peaked at 20 hours a week, and *there was no extra benefit in attending nursery full-time.*

The study found that while the benefits in cognitive learning from pre-school were real, home-raised children progressed just as well as pre-schooled children once they got to school; the ability to learn was just as great. While pre-school familiarized children with learning and helped them acquire some skills earlier, it did not especially benefit them in the long run unless their home environment was particularly lacking. In this case though – children three and over, from materially or emotionally deprived homes – it was a vital boost that would increase life chances significantly.

Penelope Leach summed up the implications of the EPPE study:

'The tendency of government policy for more day nursery provision to the exclusion of other types of childcare is extremely short-sighted; it's easier for an infant to catch up on cognitive skills later on, but they can't catch up on emotional development. The trend towards more day nurseries is out of kilter with what the research is finding.'

Madeleine Bunting, writing in the *Guardian*, saw something even more sinister – in nurseries, babies and toddlers would experience pressure to be achievers and learners at real cost to their ability to be warm and human. She summed it up as follows:

> 'For two-year-olds, think Pink Floyd: "We don't need no education." What they need is play and places to social-ize, not the government's pilot project of nursery educa-tion. Don't let the obsession with the knowledge economy of the future turn the early years into a race for cognitive skills. In the first three years, it's emotional, social and behavioural development that is absolutely crucial. Secure, happy, resilient children will catch up on the shape-sorters.'[12]

Public or private?

The UK has a mix of different kinds of nursery provision, and the EPPE study found these were far from equal in effect. In a surprising reversal of what one might expect – private day nurseries – the favourite choice of 'slammer' parents, who were often those with highest incomes, and put their children into care the youngest – had the poorest scores on all meas-ures. To quote the study's own words:

'Centres within the educational maintained/state sector generally had higher scores than those in the voluntary or private sectors. State sector educational provision was in the "good-to-excellent" range followed by local authority social services daycare. Private day nurseries were consistently found to have scores in the "minimal/adequate" range.'

The most anti-social group of children, with over 7 per cent rates of bullying, teasing and interrupting other children, came from private day nurseries.

The key finding

The most important finding was almost not mentioned because it wasn't in the brief, but it kept rearing its head all the same. The biggest effect on children's development was how loving and interested their parents were, and this was independent of income, education or social class. Here is what the EPPE report said:

'Although parents' social class and levels of education were related to child outcomes, the quality of the home-learning environment was more important and only moderately associated with social class or mothers' qualification levels. *What parents do is more important than who they are.*'

Translated into plain English, this reads: 'Love wins every time.' Or in terms of government policy: 'Look after parents of the under-threes, and they will look after their children.'

All studies have shortcomings

The interpretation of the long-term studies should not be taken on its own as the basis of your personal decision-making. These kinds of studies are poor attempts to get a grasp of incredibly complex and subtle factors. They are full of weaknesses. For instance, the NICHD study measured children's behaviour by some very rigorous standards – careful rating of videotapes of children's interaction with their mothers, for example, but also basing the children's behaviour ratings on their mothers' opinions, which would hardly be an objective measure. There may be areas of stress, harm or concern, which do not even register on these kinds of measure. In fact, there is strong evidence that this is so – the cortisol studies we will describe later have found that children under acute stress do not usually show this on the surface, appearing calm when their bodies are actually off the scale with adrenaline.

Children are extremely good at keeping up appearances. Australian researcher Anne Manne, in her book *Motherhood*, described picking up her daughter from a carer, who enthused about how well she had settled. Her daughter had a different view: 'I hated it', she stated bluntly. 'But ____ said you were happy?' 'I was crying on the inside', she replied.

Children learn quickly in group settings not to be a 'sissy', and also that when things can't be changed, they just have to endure. They are masters at telling us what we want to hear, if they sense that their views would not make any difference anyway. Children are incredibly resilient, but we should not take this for granted. (By way of parallel, it was long assumed that newborns felt little physical pain, and surgical procedures could be well tolerated. It has recently been shown they feel pain acutely, and simply go into shock so that it is not evident to observers.)

There is a strong likelihood that the most harmful effect of nursery care is simply what it lacks – that those eight minutes a day of carer attention mean children miss hours a day of intimate, playful, relaxed and stimulating times with their parents and extended family. This deficit may show up in ways the researchers had no way to measure – or did not think to ask about. The most obvious risk would be in children's own ability to parent well when they have children of their own.

The most complex and advanced of all human life skills is not maths or reading or fixing machines, it is the ability to conduct close relationships with others. This function takes up most of the new areas of the brain that differentiate us from animals. It's the reason we have a cortex. What babies learn, or fail to learn in the early years is not something measured by these studies, it is far more important. The ability to make a marriage work, to lead a team, to have the refined and subtle and tender abilities of give and take, empathy and self-awareness, these all have roots in the tiny, loving, refined interaction of mother and baby. Every extra week, month or year that a family can claw back from the demands of the economy, to keep this learning on full steam, is a lifelong plus for their child.

The one factor agreed on by all research in child development is the importance of the infant–parent bond, and how closeness of the relationship immunizes a child against present and future stresses, and enhances the development of resilient mental health.[13] If the only negative of long days spent in nursery is to weaken this connection, or prevent it ever growing, then this alone is a significant concern.

The role of politics

Government policies on childhood have a huge effect for good or ill. One suspects the Blair government had funded the EPPE study in the hope of a finding results more in line with their policies of 'everybody back to work'. The press release issued by the Minister for Children, Margaret Hodge, was a miracle of shoe-horning as it tried to honour the truth of the study and still put it in a favourable light:

'For those of us who worry – or even have pangs of guilt – about putting our children into a nursery at a young age, it's also reassuring to see the positive effect of early education on social and behavioural development when children attend particularly effective schools, and where parents are actively involved in their child's learning.'

It was still reported by several newspapers as "'No need for guilt," says minister'. But the truth of the study was quite the opposite where the under-threes were concerned – and luckily, the researchers themselves had the integrity to say so.

As a result, the government has come under increasing pressure from child development experts to prioritize extending paid parental and maternity leave rather than just invest more resources in daycare for the under-two age group. In reality, it will probably be cost factors that decide the issue. As more advanced countries than the UK have found, it is more cost effective to pay parents to raise their children, than to pay university-educated teachers, which is what is needed to achieve the good outcomes found in the study. Professor Edward Melhuish, one of the key EPPE researchers, commented:

'We know that the responsiveness of group care is much less than other childcare settings such as childminders. To improve the responsiveness of group care requires maintaining very high staff–infant ratios and keeping staff turnover down to an absolute minimum. Both are very expensive.'[14]

In fact, it is almost impossible. Turnover of nursery staff is running at 30–40 per cent per annum, caused by low pay, poor training and low status. Britain spends only 0.3 per cent of GDP on early years provision, compared with 2 per cent by Sweden. In other words, a six-fold increase in expenditure would be needed to achieve a standard which Swedish parents have decided still isn't what they want.

Melhuish told an interviewer:

'For the first 18 months to two years of life, the cost of good-quality care is potentially very high, and is comparable in cost to paid parental leave for two years. Unless you compromise on quality, the cost of subsidizing childcare for the under-twos is broadly comparable to generous parental leave.'

He used the Swedish situation to show what UK parents themselves might choose if they were allowed to:

'The Swedish case is very revealing – there was high-quality infant care available to all and heavily subsidized. It was widely used in the 70s and 80s, but in the early 90s, parental leave was increased and now there is remarkably little use of childcare under 18 months. Parents voted with their feet.'

The biggest ramification of the EPPE study was that the government's determination to get two-year-olds into nurseries was wrong. It was at least a year too soon, and positively harmful if it meant going into large group care of less than excellent quality.

Knowing the value of love

In Sydney, Australia, a famous fashion designer became doubly famous when she opted to have her nine-year-old daughter live in a separate apartment over the road in the care of a nanny, 24 hours a day. The 40-year-old had newly married, and wanted, according to the magazines which quoted her, to give the new marriage some space to find its feet. After almost a year, and after withering criticism in the media, she allowed her daughter to come and live with her again.

There have always been families where closeness is not practised and it's easy to condemn this as selfish and heartless. A more realistic explanation is that if one does not receive loving care in childhood, one simply may not understand what such care feels like, or how much it matters. Psychologist Harry Harlow's famous studies of young monkey mothers[15] raised in isolation showed this poignantly: when these female monkeys gave birth they simply ignored the newborn, leaving it to shiver and whimper alone in the corner of the cage. Only by observing and receiving nurture do primates, including humans, learn how to nurture. The social changes of the twentieth century disrupted the experiences of loving care for millions of people. The 'behavioural DNA', the skills of good parenting, can simply die out if sufficient children do not experience deep intimacy, patient care and unhurried delight in their company. Few parents would intend this to happen, but it could happen anyway.

Where to from here?

Beyond the ten or so years these studies have been following the children's lives, we just don't know what the long-term effects will be. What kind of teenagers, adults and citizens these kids will become remains to be found out. It is likely, from commonsense observation, that a different kind of childhood will make a different kind of adult.

The findings of the three studies were not all clear-cut; much that was found was confusing, suggesting unknown factors at work. The negative effects found in the NICHD study at two years of age did not manifest at three years of age, however they reappeared when the children faced the more stressful experience of starting school at five. By mid-primary school further problems arose with study skills and relationships with other children. Clearly, damage can be masked or hidden, or simply not be addressed in the questions being asked in the interviews.

What other effects might be waiting to emerge in adolescence or adulthood? Until the 20-year and 30-year studies are completed, there are so many unanswered questions. Will children raised in nursery care grow into adults who are more likely to divorce? Will they make good or poor parents? Will they even want to *be* parents? A generation of nursery-raised people are already entering their twenties. We could now begin to study in what ways they are different from other young adults raised primarily at home during their first five years.

Meanwhile, the studies reported above are now being replicated or improved on in other places worldwide. Studies in Italy, Sweden, Norway, Australia and Bermuda have all reported similar problems of early nursery care being linked to behaviour problems, and to problems in bonding with parents. The studies will continue and one day we will know much more, but for today's children that research will be too late. As parents, we have to look at the available evidence, and our own common sense, and make up our minds.

In a nutshell

- There were early concerns about the separation of children from mothers, based on the experiences of wartime.
- Early research did not find any problem with nursery care.
- In the mid-1980s, a trio of risk factors emerged – *too much, too young, for too long.*
- The effect of this trio in combination was that children who were aggressive, anxious, and had weakened relationships with their mothers.
- The 'Mummy Wars' developed between pro-work and pro-home advocates.
- Better research was needed to resolve once and for all the long-term effects.

Part Two

How a Happy Child Grows

In Part One we examined the sudden growth in full-time nursery care for babies and very young children in the UK and around the world. We saw that there were costs associated with this kind of care – negative effects on children's mental health, and on the parent–child relationship.

In the following chapters we will look at why this might be so. We will explore how a child's brain takes shape in the first three years and reveal how the three pillars of mental health – calmness, optimism and sociability – all depend on certain experiences happening at just the right time. We'll discover what an infant or toddler gets from time spent with loving parents, and whether it is possible for others – paid professional carers – to provide this.

4

Your baby's growing brain

Scientists have been studying the human brain for thousands of years, but in the last 10 years or so a breathtaking series of discoveries have taken us further forward than in all the centuries before. We are now close to solving some of the most difficult puzzles of the human condition – from schizophrenia to depression, violence to leadership, gender differences to moral development – and the biggest challenge of them all: raising good human beings.

The key to this great leap forward is a technique called Magnetic Resonance Imaging (MRI) – a technology that for the first time lets us see inside the living brain. With an MRI machine, we can actually watch the brain thinking and feeling, see where mental processes happen, and how the brain responds to different thoughts and stimuli. We can also compare one person's brain with another, and diagnose when something is missing or wrong. Best of all, we can map how the brain develops from birth right through to old age.

The second big discovery in brain science is a much humbler one – a simple swab test developed in the 1990s that is able to measure a substance in the body called cortisol.

Cortisol is a hormone produced by the adrenal glands, and is a precise indicator of the degree of stress that a person is experiencing. It is a vital substance – too little and the body will shut down and die, too much and it will virtually explode with stress. And in a great gift to stress research, cortisol levels can be measured simply by taking a wipe of saliva from a person's mouth. (Previously, only by taking a blood sample could stress be measured so accurately, and since taking a blood sample can be fairly stressful, the results were far from reliable.) Now everyone, from a crying baby to a war veteran, can have their stress monitored moment by moment. Cortisol testing is so sensitive and immediate that it can even measure the positive effects on your body of a hug or a smile.

While new technology is part of the 'great brain breakthrough', there is a third aspect – a new way of thinking that was needed to make sense of the new findings. It involved scientists talking to each other across previously unbridged boundaries, between disciplines that had little common language. On the whole, scientists are not great communicators; they usually spend their lives like moles, digging deeper into tunnels of their own speciality, with little idea of what is going on elsewhere. It is a problem that plagues medicine: for example, a doctor once told a friend of mine, 'I can't help with your knee problem – I'm a foot man!'

In the late 1990s, frustrated with this lack of interdisciplinary communication, a leading neuroscientist, Dr Allan Schore, began working to integrate the findings of the separate fields of neurology (how the brain works), biochemistry (the chemistry of the body), endocrinology (the study of hormones), child development, and psychiatry. Schore wanted to know how the behaviour we observe on the outside matches what happens on the inside of a baby's brain. Schore has an impressive brain himself, and he was able to come to grips with each of these separate fields and begin to link them together. His remarkable books[1] on the subject are so huge and complex they will never be bestsellers, but in the scientific world they unleashed great excitement, and a flood of research followed which used the new understandings to map out precisely how the human mind develops. Within five years, using the new technologies and the new 'joined up thinking', the field of neuroscience was rewriting the map of human development.[2] Today, we basically know how the human brain grows, and the best conditions for producing fully functioning human beings. And the most important ingredient arising from Schore's work and all the rest that has followed is a surprising one. What babies most need for optimal brain growth is – affection.[3]

How love grows the brain

Humans are not like most other living things. A tadpole, placed in a pond all on its own, will grow into a capable frog, and live a proper froggy life. An acorn planted miles from any other oak trees can still develop into a full-grown tree. But not so for a human baby – we are the most parent-dependent species on the face of the earth. Unless competent, caring, older people are there to help, no human baby would even learn to *walk*, let alone talk, think, feel or love.

Human babies are born with their brains relatively undeveloped, for two important reasons. The first is a practical one. If babies' heads were any bigger they would not fit through their mother's pelvis and they couldn't be born. To get around this problem, a baby's brain does two-thirds of its growing *only after it has been born*. However, in order to do this it needs the right stimulation. A baby's brain is not just mush: it cannot grow as a potato grows, by simply swelling up. It is wired more densely and intricately than any computer yet invented and this wiring has to be programmed – from experiences. A baby only grows the right parts, and wires up the right connections, if we provide the appropriate experiences for the baby at the right time.

A baby arrives with only the most basic 'software' – at birth it knows how to breathe, suck, grasp and a little else.[4] But its life is going to be far more complex than the lives of frogs or oak trees. No bundle of instincts or built-in patterns would work. Nature deals with this by leaving large parts of a child's mind blank, so it can be individually programmed to suit the kind of time and place it is growing up in. This gives the human baby – and therefore our species – the maximum flexibility to grow to adapt to its environment. From the same beginnings, we can raise a child to be a hunter on the Arctic ice, or an intensive care nurse in a British hospital. This 'programming' is such an automatic and everyday event that we take it for granted – we simply call it 'bringing a child up'. Yet it is a vast, complex and involved process, full of subtlety and the gradual addition of more and more learning, more complex than any garden, oil painting or symphony. It is a task that takes 20 years to carry out, during which literally everything we do adds to the tools a child will use to live a long and happy life.

Not all upbringings are equal, and so each human being turns out differently. Some environments are poor ones for the developing baby's mind. A baby's brain is especially sensitive to the emotional tone of its surroundings. The kind of people that a baby grows up among will greatly affect the shape and the wiring of its mental faculties. Is the family environment relaxed or aggressive? Quiet or lively? Funny or deadly serious? The baby's brain responds and grows accordingly. Early in its life, the adrenaline thermostat – the amount of adrenaline it is accustomed to, is set to handle what is a normal level of stress for that family. (This begins even during pregnancy, when a stressed mother sends stress hormones through her placenta, causing the baby's heartbeat to quicken.) By the age of six months some babies are scared all the time, others feel much more at ease. These patterns are likely to persist for a lifetime. This is the reason why in adults we see such variability in temperament and character.

This variable brain development is designed to give the baby the best chance to survive in its time and place, by matching its temperament to its circumstances. But there's a downside – it also makes the baby vulnerable if the family environment is too far from what nature intended. What if it doesn't get the right experiences to let it grow properly, to equip it for the larger world? What if the parents are depressed or drug-addicted, if the baby is never picked up and cuddled, but is just left to gaze at a TV all day, or left in a cot to stare at the ceiling? If the right things don't happen at the right time, if that child's environment is deficient in some significant way, it may not become the human being it was meant to be.

In the early 1990s, the country of Romania was opened up to the West after years of despotic rule, and a number of large orphanages were discovered where babies and children were horribly neglected. Some of these orphans were taken to the US and adopted by American families. Sadly, there were many problems, and researchers studied these children both to help them and to learn more about the effects of serious neglect. MRI scanning of these children's brains revealed shocking results. Left almost totally without affection or human interaction during the first three or four years of life, some of the children had 'black holes' in their brains where *whole areas had failed to develop.* The chances of their ever becoming fully human – sensitive, socially able, caring, non-aggressive, trusting – were remote.[5]

This is the bottom line for the human infant. No love, no stimulation, and critical areas of the brain don't grow. This knowledge puts an awesome responsibility on to us as parents and as a society. If we alter the nature of childhood from the patterns we have evolved to expect, we place our children and our future at enormous risk. Babies not only need the right experiences, but they need them at the right times. If we leave it too late, the brain-growing opportunities are lost. The damage may never be undone.

So what exactly do parents or carers need to provide? And what are the critical windows of time, the deadlines by which these ingredients have to be in place? These are important questions, so we need to examine them in detail. We can then look at whether nursery care of babies and toddlers can provide these needs, or be modified to do so more effectively.

Developing a Social Brain

A baby or toddler first learns to think by noticing that certain things happen over and over again. They learn that *this* adult is safe and friendly, and will come when it cries, smile when it smiles, reassure it when it is frightened. They learn that when *that* adult comes, they will be angry, rejecting and harsh, so it had better hush up and be quiet. By storing the strong emotional experiences linked with certain stimuli, they lay down the foundations of reasoning. They begin to develop a 'social brain' to help them meet their needs and stay out of harm's way. There is a simple test you can use to spot a secure baby – it moves its head around freely, looking about at what is going on. A baby from a frightening background lies still – its eyes move, but its head does not. It has already learned to be careful and not attract attention.

By the time your child enters toddlerhood, he or she will have become very socially skilled; able to get you to come in the night time, to find the biscuits in the cupboard, to sneak a toy when another toddler is not looking. The behavioural styles that will one day make an airline tycoon, a Nobel Peace prize winner or a prime minister are already shaping up in the sandpit.

As we have seen, it is in the first year of life that a child's emotional thermostat is set. This doesn't just affect mood or temperament, but it also has a huge effect on a child's ability to learn – to feel able to explore, concentrate, relax and delight in its environment. As adults we know that to learn well, we have to be feeling good. This means somewhere between calm and excited – the positive end of the spectrum, not scared, angry or bored. Children are just the same – a happy child learns faster and more easily and the learning reinforces the happiness, making them more exploratory and motivated in turn. The first three years of life are dense with learning and growth; more happens at this time than all the later years in expensive private schools can ever offer. Yet it is done best when a parent is simply natural, warm and playful; attempts to make babyhood 'educational' with flashcards, Japanese lessons and DVD learning programmes only make us and our babies neurotic and stressed.

Growing all the bits

The sequence of growing the brain is a fascinating one. Humans share with every other animal, bird, and fish, a primitive brain core that keeps us alive. This is our survival brain – called the amygdala, a walnut-shaped lump in the middle of our head. This part of our brain is our 'autopilot' and in a crisis it takes over. If we hear what sounds like a tiger's roar as we are walking in the woods, we no longer want to admire the scenery. Our body has a sudden urge to return quickly to the safety of our car. Your cortex – the new part of your brain – may tell you there are no wild tigers in Surrey, but your body isn't going to listen. Likewise, if you touch a burning hot plate by accident, your brain doesn't give you a chance to think about it – it takes over and jerks back your hand for you.

However, human beings are social and so we need social skills. If someone at the office mistakenly eats your doughnut, your amygdala wants to beat them about the ears, yet such behaviour isn't going to help your career. So we have developed a part of the brain called the prefrontal cortex (PFC), which is shaped like a thick band across the front part of our brain, just inside our forehead. The prefrontal cortex grows larger as we develop more social awareness – especially of what *not* to do. The PFC especially overrides impulses that might get us into trouble – to tell an unhelpful policeman what we think of them, pat an attractive person on the bottom as they walk past, and so on. The PFC is not there when we are born – it is grown between babyhood and toddlerhood. This is why, when a parents get angry with a ten-month-old baby for crying or fussing, or not eating its food, it is a useless and sad exercise. A baby has no way of knowing right from wrong, there is nowhere in its brain that yet knows how to control its behaviour. This is why we can only soothe or divert – not stop – misbehaviour at this age.

The growth of the PFC takes place in two stages. A baby loves the sound, smell and touch of its parents, or whoever gives it round-the-clock care. Just feeling, hearing and smelling these unique individuals stimulates the child's growth hormones. A child even responds to unconscious cues from the parent, such as the dilation of the pupils of a parent's eyes that show they are happy and relaxed. The growth hormones travel to the child's brain, and when they reach the 'building site' of the PFC, they stimulate more brain connections to grow there. Many other parts of the brain – with exotic names such as the orbitofrontal cortex, the hippocampus and the cingulate cortex – all grow under the effect of positive feelings arising from positive experiences. There really is such a thing as a happy brain, a brain lastingly wired to feel good, and of course there is its opposite too – the sad brain. A happy brain is more densely wired, more full of impulses. More connections mean more thinking power, and more ability to live a happy life.

In the period between six and twelve months of age, a baby's prefrontal cortex experiences a huge burst of growth. This is the age when a child is beginning to get a clear idea of who its parents are, is most fussy about strangers, and most excited at all the new games and abilities it can begin to show (such as learning to walk, and speaking its first words). This is the age when loving parents are so important. The whole first year has been a miracle – when a little child unpacks the suitcase of its life's potential, and puts everything where it is supposed to go. The brain doubles in size during this time. It will never grow as fast or as much in the rest of its lifetime. So it is vital that the right conditions are present.

The vital second year

The remarkable thing about all of the changes described so far in this chapter is that they are 'structural' – they involve the baby's brain growing new parts to carry out these new skills and tasks. Some parts of our brain are 'original equipment' – that is, they were there at birth – but a great deal is added on. You can visualize your baby's brain growing like a cauliflower in response to all the good things you and others do. Now let's look at how the right parts grow, at the right time, to give your baby self-control, and why the *second* year of life is a high-need time for responsive parenting, which cannot easily be substituted by strangers.

In the second year of life, now that the PFC has been 'installed', the self-control function that it carries out can begin to be learned. In simple terms, *in year one we learn to love, in year two we begin to learn self-control*. The process works like this: sudden or scary events – a loud noise, a frowning face – will tell the amygdala: 'Watch out, danger!' But the prefrontal cortex will say: 'Calm down, no need to panic, no need to hit out – it's just Dad with his drum kit.' The amygdala might say: 'Grab that toy, pull that child's hair, tear up the TV guide.' The prefrontal cortex will say: 'Not a good idea, Mum wouldn't like that.'

The cortex does this in an amazing way – it now has the ability to remember visual images, and so it uses a visual method of self-control. We have seen how babies are aware of faces. If a mother or father chastises a child simply by using a stronger voice to get their attention and then frowns, the child sees the frown and feels bad. The person who loves them is not happy, so they feel a temporary guilt or shame, and will usually try to deal with this by changing their behaviour. Once the parent feels appeased and satisfied that the child understands the problem, then their face shows a return of love and the child settles down.

The child takes into its own mind a picture of a disapproving parent (with an MRI you can see the visual activity firing up in the child's brain). Later, the child uses this picture memory to stop themselves stealing some cake when the parent isn't watching, or pulling out the leaves of the pot plant, or climbing on top of the TV when they have been left alone momentarily. And so a conscience is born. The prefrontal cortex is where the conscience is located, and the cortex only learns how to do this when we experience gentle but firm boundaries on our behaviour from someone who loves us deeply, and whose disapproving face matters to us enough to make us change. It doesn't happen straight away – that cake can be pretty tempting – and often there is an internal tug of war, but this is the way that children develop self-discipline until they are old enough to have their own ideas of right and wrong (usually in adolescence).

For this to work, two ingredients have to be present. Unless the toddler has a strong feeling of love and trust in an adult, then that adult's disapproval will not carry sufficient weight. The adult will have to use stronger means – hitting, punishing – to get the child to behave. The caregiver must be willing to set boundaries, give the child feedback that it is doing the wrong thing, and help it put it right, so the child can practise the ability on the inside to contain its impulses and urges. If the adults do not provide a loving and strong relationship, and a willingness to be appropriately firm, a child will continue to just follow their impulses – giving us a child of three or four who hits, hurts, grabs, steals, lies and disobeys! This is the area – aggression and disobedience – that was found to be a problem with children who had too much nursery care, too young. A carer who does not have deep emotional significance to a child will not be internalized as a source of conscience.

A child who misses out on this love/limits combination may do the right thing out of fear, but will not develop a reliable conscience about right and wrong. All little children go through a phase of being sneaky, testing out lying and the truth, but a child who is not guided by a loving carer – only by an indifferent or harsh one – does not learn self-control, only how to look good and manipulate the situation. They are in danger of becoming a charming 'con artist' rather than a person with real compassion or social concern.

The most important message of brain development for the second year of life is that only those who love a child can teach them to have self-discipline. Others can frighten a child into behaving well, but the child is then likely to become sneaky, and cunning in response. Only someone who loves you can help you to grow a conscience that is guiding, but not crushing, and moderated by love and balance. (It is interesting to note that the Christian religion is based on this loving parent idea – that the God of the New Testament is never punishing or destroying, but always loves us and will welcome us back. And sure enough, research finds that Christians, along with Buddhists and other compassion-based religions, have better physical and mental health.)

How stories feed the brain

It is not hard to see how the things that parents do feed the brain and heart of their baby and toddler. A well-loved child simply radiates joy and excitement at being alive. A child whose father tells them a story as they lie in bed last thing before going to sleep, receives multiple gifts: they feel special and loved, they relax and their imagination soars. The words read in their father's familiar tones, with a few funny voices thrown in, paint pictures in the child's mind. They will relish this and request repeat performances, not wanting the excitement to stop.

Inside the brain of the toddler, the left side, which hears the words, is sending messages across to the right side, which makes the mental pictures. Both halves of the brain are linked by a small area of 'cabling' called the corpus callosum, which is larger in girls than boys, and which is vital for being able to express oneself easily and quickly. This pipeline will only grow if it is used. Through listening to stories, new connections are wired up, ensuring the toddler will become a child who can quickly move from thoughts to words, express feelings clearly and reason things out, as well as have a vivid and pro-active imagination. There will also be links growing down into the emotional, 'primitive' parts of the brain, which say things like: 'This reading business is so cool, it's comforting, exciting, and makes my mind feel good.' It is deeply associated with the voice, the arms and the comfort of a parent who is willing to relax and enjoy this special moment of time. A love of books, thinking and human contact, are all growing together.

It is beautiful to watch good parenting in action, something you can see every day in homes, shopping centres, parks and bus stops. A mother or father chatters to their child casually and easily as they go about their activities, explaining what they are doing, occasionally giving a more stern directive but mostly enjoying the company of their child. It is very physical – they may give in to an urge to nuzzle, tickle or squeeze their child, or excite them with a toy or something that comes to hand. The child's hand nestles in the parent's as they go on their way. It is all effortless and natural. How delightful the world of a child is, with this kind of easy, interested, warm enjoyment on tap.

Poor parenting is also easy to find. Walk down the high street and you will notice parent–child pairs with no apparent warmth or connection at all: a parent striding impatiently ahead as their toddler struggles to keep up. Every parent has their impatient moments, but imagine being a child who continually senses that they are a nuisance to their only source of love, never feeling welcome, valued or important. It's distressing to watch parents who have almost no empathy or time for their child, almost radiating resentment at having their life so inconvenienced. Hurried or half-hearted parenting is self-defeating since a neglected and hurried child will become so much more of a problem as they progress into behaviour problems at school, a nightmare adolescence and an horrific adult life. It is so much easier to make friends with our children, decide to enjoy them, and by giving ourselves to them, get so much back in the long run.

In a nutshell

- MRI brain scanning shows us that the brain of a child develops most after it is born, through stimulation in the first three years.
- Loving interaction stimulates the baby's brain to grow more connections, and the areas that will help it feel safe and connected.
- During the time between six and twelve months, the prefrontal cortex grows as a response to nurturing, giving the child the ability to regulate emotions and relate to other people.
- From 12–24 months, self-control is internalized and can only come from the loving firmness of someone important to the child.
- Loving interaction feeds our child's brain, and it learns to think best when it is happy and unafraid.

5

How babies teach
us to parent

Nature looks after young parents. When our babies are born, however many parenting books we might have read, we are still clueless and awkward. It's only through spending time with our child, that we gradually learn its signals, and come to relax and trust our reactions. In this chapter, we will look at how subtle, special, and intense this interaction is, and how much is lost if the parent child relationship is compromised or neglected.

Only a tiny part of our parenting behaviour is instinctive. We are programmed to see all large-eyed soft furry creatures as cute. (That is why sales of teddy bears outrank sales of plastic toads!) But instinct is not enough; it provides only an urge, and not the fine detail of how to nurture. We acquire the considerable skills needed for parenthood in three ways.

Firstly, it arises from the nurturing we received as a child – if we were loved as babies, we respond more warmly, and more capably, to babies as an adult. We feel comfortable and calm around crying, needy babies because deep inside us is the memory that this can soon be remedied. Loving feelings are triggered.

Secondly, we get parenting skills from being around babies and parents as we were growing up – if we saw parents dealing with babies, and perhaps even helped or imitated them with our own younger brothers and sisters, then these skills would have been naturally acquired. (This was easier in the big families of the past, where almost everyone had six or seven brothers or sisters and lots of practice – today one-third of new parents have never even held a baby before their own is born.)

The third way in which parenting skills are acquired is through sheer determination and loving intentions, which through trial and error lead us to find out what works. Many parents today are good parents simply because they were determined to do the best they could.

Baby helps, too

A baby does its part to help us, too. Their emotional communication encourages us to get it right. A laughing baby makes us continue our antics to make it laugh some more. A crying baby makes us want to soothe it and make it happy and quiet again. What is clear from the research is that a baby needs a *human* response – a tube bringing milk, or a heater giving warmth, or a machine to jiggle and stimulate it is not enough. (It's been tried!) Since this baby is to live among humans, and not just machines, it needs humans to teach it. Only real people – consistent, responsive, interested people – can give the refined and complex responses a baby needs.

In the 1980s some researchers used ultra high-speed film cameras (the kind used to show bullets in mid-air) to record mothers and babies interacting. This film, slowed down to show every tiny movement, reveals an extraordinary dance of eye contact, slight facial movements, raised eyebrows, little sounds which bounce to and fro between mother and child. It is these little signals that say a thousand times a day: 'I'm here', 'I'm noticing', 'I care about you'. Some of these signals are so subtle, and so fast, that even with the most sophisticated cameras, it is impossible to see who moves first – mother and baby seem almost telepathically co-ordinated.

This level of rapport, or empathy between parent and child is not automatic, it arises little by little. The baby educates the parent, and the parent educates the baby. Gradually, parent and child learn each other's language, and shape each other into a more and more finely-tuned partner in the parenting endeavour. The eventual result of all this interaction – the soothing, the stimulating, the directing – is that the growing child gradually becomes less needy. It learns, through our soothing, gradually to soothe itself. Through our happiness, it learns how to be happier and more excited. Through our caring reassurance, it learns not to be so afraid of pain or change. By being so much 'there' for our babies, we actually make them more independent later on. They have us so deeply in their bones that they can draw on this even when we are not around.

We are only now learning just how much the baby's body needs this input. Touching and stroking, a smiling face, a laughing voice, all feed the baby just as much as the nutrients in its mother's milk. This isn't just poetic language – each of these stimuli triggers measurable surges in the baby's growth hormones, its skin and muscle tone, and speeds up the growth of nerve cells in the brain.

Mother–baby connections

Researchers have begun to find that in many important ways, a new baby is still a part of its mother's body. Her breast milk not only feeds the baby, but keeps it immune from illness with her antibodies. Her touching and cuddles releases growth hormone, so that the baby's body, including its brain, continues to grow. Her calming touch and warmth and attention dissolve the stress hormones that sweep through its body.

The baby also changes the mother's chemistry. When a woman gives birth, the hormone prolactin is released in her body. This stimulates breast milk to be produced, and when the baby suckles; this sends a signal to the mother's body that 'there really is a baby here' and the prolactin levels rise higher still. Prolactin particularly affects the mother's brain, making her feel both more tender-hearted and more peaceful. Women joke about this effect: 'I stopped caring about fashion!' 'I didn't care about a tidy house!' 'I didn't want to be CEO of my organization. I just wanted to be with the baby.'

It is possible that the coldness felt and shown by some mothers in the 1950s and 1960s was a result of the extremely low rates of breastfeeding in that era, as milk companies and health workers touted artificial formulae as the modern way to go. Bottle-feeding mothers would have missed out on the prolactin boost that helps maternal feelings to 'kick in'. Little wonder that by the late 1960s there was a huge swing back towards affection, intimacy and 'all you need is love'.

I feel your pain

Part of the phenomena of being a mother or father, which no other adult person shares towards a baby in quite the same way, is the 'identification' with the baby's feelings. Its pain is your pain, and you are uniquely motivated to soothe it.

The mother of an upset baby reacts by entering into the distress that the baby feels, hopefully without being overwhelmed – she feels for her baby, but also knows it can be helped. This is a very physical thing – the sound of a crying baby at the cinema or in a restaurant can cause other mothers to leak milk spontaneously. The sympathetic reaction is just the first step as it unleashes a whole chain of caring responses. Videotaped studies show the same identical pattern in every human society. It is quite unconscious and seems to happen naturally. Firstly, if the baby is crying loudly, the mother will speak loudly, matching its volume, and also mirroring its look of distress in her own face. Her words will be kind, 'Oh, what's the matter then?' but in a strong enough voice that the baby takes notice even above its own distress and feels her connection. The mother then 'leads' the baby out of distress by progressively calming down her own voice, talking to the baby in a gradually quieter way, making crooning noises which act to steady the baby's heartbeat, quieten its cries, and send its cortisol levels coasting back down to rest.

This is a lifelong skill – spouses settle each other down, wise elders calm down hot-headed youths, leaders reassure their people. It always follows the same two stages – empathizing with their upset by mirroring it themselves, but then leading them to calmness. In the *Lord of the Rings*' final battle scenes, Aragorn rallies his hopelessly outnumbered horsemen. He begins his rousing speech *not* by saying: 'There's nothing to fear' or 'We will win' but by saying 'I see in your eyes the same fear that would take the heart of me …' From this point of shared understanding ('I am just like you') he goes on to inspire their courage to be of good heart in the worthiness of their cause.

The pattern between mother and child happens totally without thought. A mother knows the baby's distress won't 'take the heart of her' because she has (hopefully) reserves of calm ways to ease the distress; she knows that these things will pass. When a parent does not have this inner resource from their own babyhood experiences, the results can be catastrophic. A distressed and lonely mother may collapse in depression. A new boyfriend, lacking the early bonding to the child, and troubled by his own memories from a neglected babyhood, may shake the child violently and injure or even kill it. It is clear that in vulnerable families, many external resources must be brought to bear. This could be a husband who takes over so his partner can rest and regain her spirits;

an infant health nurse who comforts and reassures the mother that her baby is fine; a mother's friendship group, where she can laugh and relax, know that everyone has these terrible moments, see that others have come through the same or worse, and understand that she will not be abandoned to struggle alone. We all need to feel 'held' by others, so we can relax and care for our baby well.

Does parenthood change your brain?

We know that parenting changes a baby's brain – but what about the reverse? Researchers suspect this might be so – that interacting with a baby triggers structural changes which make it easier to be a parent and to do it well.

Hormonal changes occur in both mothers and fathers, and it is likely that over the next five years it will be confirmed that by spending time with a baby, a new parent undergoes biochemical and then structural changes in their brain, increasing empathy, strength of love, ability to notice and respond, and a lessening of self-absorption. As it stands, most parents describe feeling these changes subjectively. The biggest changes are a shift of focus from self to baby – the clear sense that you would give your life for your child.

The prolactin effect changes a breastfeeding mother's state of mind to make her more tender, patient and focused on her child. Fathers of new babies experience lower levels of testosterone, so that they are gentler and more relaxed. Spending time caring for babies makes fathers less likely to harm them, more likely to decline career changes that impair family well-being, and even less likely to seek divorce.

The critical question becomes: if a parent has little time with their baby or toddler, do they fail to make these changes, and consequently have more difficulty as an effective parent? The research findings from NICHD and EPPE that weak infant–mother bonds are made even weaker by too much early daycare might be explained by the mother not having enough baby exposure in the daytime hours to allow her brain to make this transition.

Strength comes from good beginnings

To conclude, in the first two years, babies seem to do best if given enormous amounts of care and attention from a small, stable group of adults and siblings. Investing this time makes for an easier life, since in childhood and adolescence, the child will be more sociable, calm, and easy to deal with if babyhood has gone well.

It all comes down to time. Only time allows you to give your full attention. Whether between husband and wife, or parent and child, you know you are loved when the other person 'only has eyes for you'. The news from brain studies is that loving time spent with babies is doing vital things, hidden out of sight inside your babies growing brain. Allan Schore described the building of a baby's brain as a co-operative effort between baby and parent. In the interactions, the pathways are laid down, the grey matter grows richer and denser. The infant develops – not by any effort to 'educate' them but in the tender, sensitive and warm way that someone who loves the baby just naturally coos, plays, tickles, talks to and comforts it when it's upset. A hunter-gatherer mother in the Kalahari does this just the same as a mother in a Manhattan apartment or a single father on a remote island in Scotland. Emotionally healthy adults do these things without knowing why or what they are doing, except that it is likely that someone did it for them too, and so on back through time immemorial. Babies naturally fascinate adults, and adults naturally delight babies, and this dance of fascination and fun sets their brains to growing in just the way that will work best to produce a positive member of the human race.

A long line of mothers

Australian psychiatrist Dr Peter Cook has created a vivid picture of how to see mothering in perspective. He asks that you first imagine yourself, standing with your child in your arms. Imagine, your own mother standing behind you, with her arms about you, and her mother (your grandmother) standing behind her. In most families this is the spread of mothers who have been alive at the same time and known each other well. They would form a line a little less than a metre long (unless obesity runs in your family, in which case it would be two metres!). Now, if we add the mother of your grandmother, and her mother, and continue going back in time for all the years that human beings have been on the earth, you would see a line of mothers stretching for something like 50 miles. And every one of these mothers would have been successful, competent enough to make sure that their own daughter survived at least to be able to bear a child. Those who did not make it did not have their lines continue. It's an awe-inspiring picture – you are descended from a long, long line of successful mothers (and fathers). And the skill and dedication with which they raised their children is now in your muscles, sinews and nerves. It's literally in your hands. You are the link in this chain, and all the parents and children whose lives lie in the future depend on your being able to pass on these skills and qualities to them. Human loving is a heritage of impressive proportions.[1]

Feelings colour thinking

The structure of the brain determines absolutely the way we experience our world. All experiences we have must flow through the same primitive pathways. Everything we experience comes in first through the senses. Next, before it can be considered by our 'thinking brain', our experience passes through the emotional layer deep down inside the brain. Only last of all does it move outward to the thinking brain, the cortex, which is like a shell on the outside. Everything experienced in life carries a feeling tone with it. Our experience of life is filtered by our feelings, so when someone you like gives you some information, you are more likely to think:

'What a great idea.' Just seeing them has already set a receptive emotional frame of mind into motion, before thinking can take place.

Your emotional tone is programmed in early life to have a certain 'flavour' so that you see the world as predominantly a good, fun place, or a scary and uncertain one. And because of the way the brain is wired, this colours everything you experience from then on.

Everyone knows how mood affects perceptions. When you are depressed, you seem to notice all the gloomy and depressing things in the world around you. The news is all bad. All TV programmes are rubbish. You fight with your partner. Your life seems pointless. This in turn makes you even more depressed. On the other hand, when you are feeling good, the world looks good. Remember being in love? Everything takes on a rosy hue: street lamps and buildings, old people, children, dogs and cats all seem radiant and beautiful.

We know we can alter our mood, and work on our attitude. But early childhood experiences determine the range through which we can swing, so that some people go from feeling anxious to just feeling okay, and never any higher. Others can move from calm right through to exuberant and joyful, and are only rarely sad or depressed. Yet others fly into a sudden rage with alarming speed. These tendencies are enduring, they become part of the person's character, written into the very lines on their face, the stoop of their shoulders and how deeply they allow themselves to breathe.

Babyhood is where you develop your attitude to life. Of course, temperament comes into it – some babies are born shy and quiet, and others are born loud and brave. But as parents, we can shape if they are *happily* quiet or *happily* brave. We set the emotional tone of their lives.

Don't forget the fun

Finally, a parent's job is not just to calm a child, but also to excite it. A happy parent also stimulates a baby into laughter and delight, effectively regulating its mood upwards into more activity and alertness. Parents and older siblings love to stir babies up, and be rewarded with their chuckles of delight. A baby that is listless, depressed or bored, will sparkle and speed up its reactions if an adult comes along to tickle it, play peek-a-boo, show it a colourful and noisy toy. In this way a mother or other caregiver (fathers tend to be rather good at this) improve the child's mood, and also raise its tolerance for greater levels of arousal. They can show the child that a fast heartbeat and bit of movement and change are fun, not frightening. These activities are intelligence building, and they help a child develop more aliveness and mental and physical condition. The best thing we can do for our babies is always to enjoy them.

In a nutshell

- The first and most important thing a mother helps a baby to develop is calming skills – and it grows brain structures to be able to do this, if she is successful.
- The mother's chemistry (and probably the father's too) is changed by her interactions with the baby.
- Stimulation, fun and excitement also help a baby, so that they learn both to calm down and to liven up, from the interest and vitality of their caregiver.

Babies and emotional intelligence

All babies develop in the same age-old sequence. Things have to happen in the right order. When a baby first emerges from the womb, its brain is mostly dedicated to *sensing*. Because of this, a newborn knows only simple things – whether it is cold or warm, hungry or full, cuddled or left alone. But quite rapidly, in the first weeks and months of life, these *sensations* start to become refined into *emotions*. For instance, if a baby is left cold and hungry for too long, if it is not touched by warm, comforting skin, it becomes lonely and scared. If cuddled, smiled and sung to, it becomes happy; talked to and tickled and jiggled, it becomes excited.

The formation of these separate emotions helps the baby to communicate – *by expressing emotions, a baby can better get its needs met from the adults nearby.* This is because the adults caring for the baby understand these emotions – they have them too. Emotions are the first human language. It is the demonstration of *our* feelings, responsively given, that teach a child how to express its feelings *in ways that will succeed.* If a baby shows emotions, a caring empathic adult will almost automatically do what is needed to meet its needs. By this we mean emotional needs – not just providing food or warmth, but to make the child happy, excited, or calm, as the situation requires.

Avoiding extremes

When parents get things wrong, it is usually in one of two ways. A danger arises if the parent or carer is overstressed, busy, or the opposite – depressed and lethargic. Both of these conditions mean the baby will be neglected. A baby may have to show extreme behaviour – agitation, rage or distress – in order to elicit the response it needs. This may become a pattern that lasts into its adult life – creating an adult who is chronically anxious, or prone to rage, or volatile and over-emotional under stress – since these were the only emotions that succeeded when they were in their formative years.

An apathetic, withdrawn carer who doesn't make eye contact and leaves their baby alone a lot leads to a more depressed baby with a less active left brain, not so good at thinking, and at risk of emotional problems in adulthood. The actions of an angry or resentful carer, who picks up the baby harshly or with sudden movements, and who doesn't match her timing to the baby's signals, will lead to a child who is poorly attached, doesn't form close bonds in adult life, and is disorganized and awkward.

Often today, a baby is left in its cot much more than was the case in hunter-gatherer societies, where babies were almost always carried on a hip or in a sling, and usually slept with their mothers at night (though not on a big soft mattress, but more often in a hammock or on a mat). With the new distance between parent and child in the modern world, and the busyness of parents, the idea of a 'good' baby is one that is quiet all the time, or sleeps for long periods. Yet what passes for 'good' in a nursery or home setting, might indicate a depressed baby, or one that is lonely and bored, and soothes itself by shutting down its feelings. If 'good' means 'convenient', then there may be problems brewing.

How a baby learns emotional regulation

Love grows a baby, and it also teaches a baby vital things. In the first two years of life, a baby learns from its parents how to *regulate* its emotions. It is natural and important for a baby to experience all the negative emotions – fear, sorrow, frustration; but essential too that they are not left feeling that way for too long or too often.

The critical point for a mother or father to understand is that *a baby does not have the ability, on its own, to manage its emotions.* If frightened or lonely, a baby's anxiety levels, as measured by its cortisol, go through the roof. When a parent comes to soothe and cuddle them, the baby's levels of cortisol can be seen to coast quickly back to normal. But if comfort does not come reliably or soon, the levels of stress may remain continually high for hours, and if this happens often enough, the baby's adrenaline thermostat reset itself to a higher level. They become permanently stressed. Just as we have to keep a baby warm – since it cannot regulate its own temperature – we also have to keep it comforted emotionally, as it cannot regulate its own stress.

Visitors to the surviving Neolithic societies in remote parts of the world often notice something quite remarkable in the igloos, yurts and grass huts of their hosts – the infants in these societies hardly ever cry. On closer study, anthropologists have found that the infants in these cultures begin 'getting ready' to cry, but the adults are so alert and responsive to their needs that they are calmed before the actual crying can begin. Resolution comes quickly. (Parents in these societies also know the little signs that tell when their babies are about to poo or wee, very helpful in a world without nappies.)

Parents who are warm and responsive – in whatever culture they may live – by acting promptly and caringly, teach their baby that expressing feelings leads to a solution. Somebody will be there to 'kiss it better'. If parents or carers do not come soon, to soothe and settle, then it is a different story. Persistent fear, persistent loneliness, will cause stress chemicals to be released in the baby's body, as its biology tells it: 'Something is badly wrong here.' The stress chemicals have a markedly negative effect if allowed to persist for long. They block growth hormones, shutting down the growth of the baby, both mentally and physically. Stressed babies do not waste energy on growing. Only when happiness, laughter and peace prevail, will growth and development recommence.

The reverse is equally true – when a baby sees a smiling face, or is given a warm cuddle, its body produces more growth hormone, its brain comes alive, and grows new connections more quickly. Happiness is as essential to a baby as food or air.

• • •

To sum up, the whole emotional experience a baby has with its parents shapes its personality in three ways.

- Patterns of feeling – how to communicate emotions and get its needs met.
- The emotional mood of the home sets a baby's emotional thermometer – the baby 'decides' deep in its nervous system, whether life is basically good, safe and fun, or bad, scary and dangerous.
- A cared-for baby develops a more resilient self. It experiences bad times as unlikely to last long, so it has optimism, endurance and hope.

What emotional intelligence is

We know that a baby's brain grows through interaction, and that it grows upwards like tree, from sensing trunk to feeling limbs to thinking branches. In the ideal human being, all three affect each other and help each other to work well. From this idea – that the best thinking includes our emotions – has come the concept of emotional intelligence, which in recent years has swept the world of psychology, education and management. It has changed our very idea of what makes a good person. A century ago, parents wanted their children to have good manners and social graces so as to rise up the social ladder. In the post-war decades the big thing was education. But today's parents want their offspring to be emotionally intelligent. In a sense this is rediscovering ancient wisdom: Jesus, Buddha, Gandhi and Mother Teresa were emotionally alive, heartfelt and yet thinking and highly intelligent people. Their feelings informed and drove their thinking, but never overrode it.

Almost everyone knows someone who is extremely intelligent but at the same time hopeless in social situations, and prone to making unwise life choices. Intelligence on its own does not guarantee wisdom. Conversely we all know people of very modest intellectual ability who are nonetheless warm, wonderful and wise. These people are good to be around, and the things they do are usually successful. To get on well in life, whatever your ability, it helps to be calm, warm, strong and positive, and have good people skills. These qualities are learned early in childhood, by the time they arrive in the school playground some children are evidently friendly, sociable, and easy going, while others are insecure bullies or awkward and shy. The early years matter so very much for emotional learning.

Emotions are our friends

Brain science shows that emotions, when working as they should, are not troubling storms, but a significant help to our intellect. The emotional parts of our brain are directly wired to our senses, and so will often tell us something important from subtle cues, long before our logic can work it out. Einstein described this emotional sense that told him where to look for a solution, and most of us have experienced it to some degree. It is often called a sixth sense, but it is really just allowing your brain to notice and react to small cues that don't yet add up to a whole. An uneasy emotion can tell us that something or someone is amiss – dangerous, or in danger – long before we have actual proof of this. It is only later that we figure out that we were right although we knew it 'in our heart' long before.

Emotions are not always our friends though. To the degree that our emotions are not steady and at peace, our thinking can easily be distorted and disturbed. We may suffer from paranoid and exaggerated fears, explosive anger, obsessive focus on some trivial matter; we can worry our whole life away. If the emotional part of the brain has been habituated in babyhood to fear and uncertainty, and has not grown those compartments of the brain which self-soothe and which self-control the impulses coming from inside, then a person may find themselves experiencing emotional distress, with no real reason in the outer world. We worry about our children learning piano or maths, when the really important lessons – happiness, calm and optimism – can be totally neglected or even damaged by our misplaced efforts.

Why emotional intelligence matters

The emotional development that takes place in the first three years is more important than any other aspect of a child's growing up. It is far more influential on later life success than academic or intellectual intelligence. (According to recent studies, intelligence only predicts about 20 per cent of career or financial success, whereas emotional intelligence – the ability to deal well with your own feelings and those of others – predicts around 80 per cent.) Emotional intelligence is at the root of our effectiveness as people. Emotional literacy is our first language, and it will always be our most important one. When as an adult we are able to communicate our feelings to our partner, co-ordinate a team of people at work, or stay calm while listening to the anger of our teenager whose feelings we have hurt, we are drawing on this emotional ability that began in the first few months of life. As we grow older the process still continues; we learn to recognize more subtle degrees of emotion, and can make better and better 'calls' on how to handle people. Eventually, this becomes what we commonly call 'wisdom'.[1]

There's a deep irony here. While a businessman or woman works into the night, earning the money to afford an expensive school, the small, caring interactions between the hired nanny and a baby will be determining if that baby will one day be a caring friend or a damaged and difficult loner.

The great part of nature's built-in plan for babies is that it is designed to work without great effort or artifice. Parenting is not rocket science. You don't have to be a super-parent, trying to 'stimulate' your baby or give it 'early learning' – and if you tried it, would just mess things up. The things we naturally do with babies – play, talk, comfort, smile – are the best things we can do; they are the essential brain food, given in just the right emotional tone. Many parents who hand over the care of their baby to a stranger do so because they have no idea how much is going on in these early months. They assume that it is enough for someone to feed and change a baby's nappy, cuddle it if it cries, and just 'wait for it to grow up'. Nothing could be further from the truth.

Help me with my world!

To grow up in optimal mental health, a baby needs three specific things from reasonably functional adults. These are:

1. Loving soothing;
2. Loving firmness;
3. Loving fun and excitement.

Of course, wise parents have always known this. What is new, what MRI imaging has shown us, is that these inputs actually develop areas within the brain – just like watering the garden, these ingredients at the right time cause neural areas to blossom and grow.

How does it happen?

So how does a baby develop the ability to be emotionally intelligent, calm, happy and strong? It happens in stages. At first the baby sees only a confused blur around it, but soon starts to take in the world of sights and smells and sounds, and to recognize patterns. Faces are the first thing it notices – babies are programmed to notice faces out of all the other shapes and colours in the world around them, and girl babies do this slightly more than boys. A baby's eyes are prefocused at just the distance from its mother's breast to her face – the perfect distance for a loving gaze of 'Thanks, Mum!' After a month or two of happy gazing, babies do a remarkable and wonderful thing – they form the image in their mind of their mother's face, and can remember it when she is not there. They will eventually have a mental photo gallery of the moods and expressions of those people it knows best. It might be a smiling parent coming to soothe them when they cry, or a frowning harsh parent impatient and angry at being disturbed; the baby's body reacts accordingly. They not only have these mental snapshots, but they use them rather in the way a soldier might look at a photo of his girlfriend to feel less lonely in his foxhole. By using their newly developing visual brain, babies can summon up the experience of their parents and use this as a resource to help them feel better. (As we will learn later, they can also use it to restrain themselves – they remember the stern face of their mother or father, to stop themselves doing something that they know is wrong.)

The greatest danger to a young baby's mental health, just as for an adult, is unrelieved anxiety. Unable to calm itself, a baby's body floods with cortisol, and this makes it feel worse still. Babies were not designed to be away from someone's arms for very long, and at this age they need an external source of reassurance that everything is okay. An abandoned baby will cry for a short time in great alarm, but then it will quieten itself – this is probably an instinct to avoid being noticed by predatory animals. However, its anxiety level will remain sky high. It might look like it is being a 'good' baby, but it has just gone into a self-protective, numbed state. So calming and settling – coming quickly to a baby's help – is the first function a parent needs to be able to fulfil.

Studies of nursery staff in even the best centres are unsettling in this regard: they indicate that their interactions with children are brief, there is much less eye contact, comfort is given fleetingly, conversations are just a few words – 'That's nice' – not the long lingering interactions that happen between parent and child. Researchers have noted that children's overtures, especially the subtle ones given by a baby with its eyes and soft noises, to 'notice me', are often completely ignored.[2]

A new definition of love

A baby learns by interaction, and the interaction needs to be intense and familiar – the word that researchers use again and again in their writing is 'responsive'. This means that *a person caring for a baby or young toddler has to love it, if that child is to grow as it should.* It is as simple, stark and obvious as that. In a sense this whole body of new research has pinpointed an operational definition of what love really is – *it is the giving of detailed attention and time.* When we love someone, we are deeply attentive to them, and we put their needs ahead of our own. This is the difficulty in having the parenting role taken over by salaried carers, dealing with children en masse. Carers can care, but they rarely love. Love cannot be bought, it can't even be willed. It has to be felt. It has to be unique to those two people. And it has to grow naturally over time.

From the feeling to the thinking brain

We have seen how a baby progresses from sensing its world, to having feelings and learning from adults how to manage these feelings. This is only the first step – what happens next is the most astounding part of the story. From feelings, a child learns to think. In order to solve the emotional problems of living, its brain develops the ability to reason, the child begins its long journey to becoming a calm, thoughtful individual who can take into account the needs of others as well as itself.

Feelings are the engines that drive our thinking along and give it a reason to happen. The importance of this cannot be overstated since it is a complete reversal of how the brain was understood until only just recently. Scientists, including doctors and psychiatrists, used to think that emotions were irrelevant – a part of our animal self that we would be better off without. This led to the massive use of medication and alcohol to dampen emotions rather than deal with them. But feelings are not just emotional static, they literally are at the heart of our intellect. Again, the evidence comes from how the brain is wired. MRI scans reveal that the emotional parts of the brain are directly connected upwards and outwards into the thinking parts, as the branches of a tree spread out from the lower limbs and the trunk. Thinking has its basis in feeling, and the two inform and help each other. This interconnection develops intensively in babies from six months through to the age of two.

To sum up, no one needs love as intensely as a newborn baby. Loving a baby ensures the fine detailed attention, the intense responsiveness that actually sculpts the baby's brain and smoothes out its emotions and enables it to think calmly, happily and well. Only a well-loved baby can reach its full potential as a human being. It seems too important a thing to place in jeopardy unless there are life and death reasons to do so.

In a nutshell

- By interacting with parents, it develops an emotional language, and uses emotions to communicate its needs.
- As parents or carers respond to its emotions, it then learns to regulate them, parents provide the regulation until the child learns to do this for itself.
- Being emotionally intelligent, and able to love and trust, are the first lessons a baby learns for a lifetime of happiness.
- The early months and years are about learning to love – the most important skills of all for a human lifetime.

Why nursery doesn't work for babies

It is time now to look more closely at the situation in nursery care. First, let's begin with what common sense can tell us. Nursery carers are almost all women. They tend to be young and not yet have children of their own. Because of the low levels of pay, generally they do not have a high level of education – some may have some college qualifications in childcare, others none at all. (The better qualified staff in nurseries are more likely to be administering the centre than directly caring for the children.)

This in itself does not necessarily mean that the care given will be poor. In all human societies young people often care for babies, and at least a nursery is a sociable setting, less isolated than working as a nanny or a babysitter. However, it would be a very special young person who would not find spending all day every day with a group of little children to be wearing and boring after a while.

What the research says

To find out in an objective way what kind of interaction children receive from nursery-care workers, detailed observational studies have been carried out in nurseries and daycare centres in many parts of the world. Using video cameras and one-way mirrors, trained observers have rated the interaction quality between carers and children. Sadly, the results are not good. Even when childcare workers know that they are being observed as they go about their work – when presumably they are giving it their best – they do not do as good a job as parents. There are far fewer intimate exchanges between carers and children than offered by parents, and interactions are more mechanical, brusque and shorter in duration. They are simply not as responsive.[1]

All human babies have a specific behaviour that they use to elicit love and attention. Hundreds of times, in the course of the normal day, a healthy baby will 'seek' his mother with his eyes, while at the same time speaking or making sounds to her. The mother almost always responds by looking round, making eye contact with the baby even from some distance away, and offers some friendly words back. It is the beginning of human conversation, and the interesting thing is that the child is almost always the initiator and the mother or father almost always the responder. Only depressed or exhausted parents do not do so, and this symptom is a cause for alarm and intervention when it occurs. In nursery-care settings, however, observers notice that more than half of the time (sometimes much more than that) the carers simply do not see these 'reachings out' by the child (who is often restrained in a high chair or cot), and soon the child gives up and gazes listlessly or plays repetitively with a spoon or toy instead. Soon the child no longer tries to be sociable. A trained observer would probably label such a child as 'depressed'. In a setting where the adults are busy, this child is more likely to be labelled 'good' and to get even less of the carer's time than if they made a fuss.[2]

This is not the fault of the carer – in most cases they try their best to be good surrogate parents, but there are two significant factors working against them. They are not the parent of the child, and they rarely have a long-term stable relationship with them. Both child and carer are just passing through each other's lives. It would be a cause of grief for either to care too much for the other, and both need to withhold their feelings for their own self-protection. More prosaically, it is a job with shift changes and often frequent changes of employment, so it is difficult to develop the really fine knowledge and skill with any individual child. Some guidelines for nursery carers specify that: 'They should maintain eye contact with each baby, even when they are feeding or changing another baby,' which is clearly so impossible as to be ridiculous. A nursery situation never has a one-to-one ratio of carer to baby – it would be prohibitively expensive. The best nurseries have one carer to three babies, and often this is one to five or six when carers are filling in forms, taking a break, or performing other duties. So the child gets only a fraction of the time and energy that it ideally needs.

What cortisol tells us about nursery stress

A nursery environment is stressful for babies and toddlers; we know this because it can be measured with cortisol testing. A baby left at a nursery will often show significantly higher levels of cortisol than at home with its parent. The reasons for this are not hard to figure out. Babies do not have a sense of time; they cannot understand that 'in eight hours' time my mother will be back'. Indeed, they are programmed to assume that if their beloved caregiver leaves them, they are in danger. Their body escalates into full panic. A responsive and alert caregiver can soothe the baby and lower its cortisol levels, but this requires a good relationship and lots of time. Recently, some US researchers found that cortisol levels in a child at home are highest in the morning – the exciting part of the day – and gradually fall away as the day goes on, but in a nursery, they actually rise as the day goes on.[3]

A Cambridge University study released in 2005 reported these alarming results:

'Toddlers starting at childcare experience high levels of stress in the first weeks after separating from their parents ... Hormone levels doubled even in secure youngsters during the first nine days of childcare ... The levels fell over time but five months later were still significantly higher than for infants of the same age who stayed at home.'[4]

An important learning from this study was that at five months the children were felt to have settled in well, *since they showed no outer signs of distress*. But the cortisol readings showed that on the inside they were still frightened and ill at ease. It is a consistent observation in all the cortisol studies that children appear to cope with stress after time, only because they have learned to cover up. Reassurance that 'they are fine' simply is not accurate.

Study leader Professor Michael Lamb warned that children spending the day in a nursery would need more time for soothing and reassurance at the end of the day to return their stress levels to normal. Without that comfort from a parent, they could start the next day 'hyperaroused'. Professor Lamb recommended minimizing the amount of time children had to spend in care, and that nurseries have more regular rest periods and peaceful environments to allow children to self-calm.

The reality gap

At the heart of the daycare problem is the gap between the ideal and the reality. Today's highly commercialized nursery industry wraps its product in a rosy glow of feel-good propaganda. Nurseries have cute names such as Peter Pan's Place, Teddy Bear's Castle, and Happy Land. The terminology is continuously being updated – what was in the 1970s a child-minding centre, in the 1980s became a childcare centre and today is called an early learning centre, each stage matching the changing anxieties of each generation of parents. In the US, daycare centres sound pragmatic and efficient; in the UK, nursery names have the warm, fuzzy connotations of Mary Poppins. The UK's leading nursery chain cleverly manages to cover all the bases with its corporate motto – Safe, Loved and Learning. What more could a parent ask for? Sadly, the second of these seems to me an impossibility. Whilst individuals may be very caring, love is the one thing in the whole world that a corporation cannot provide.

Childcare was once a community-based, idealistic sector, but it has changed into something very different. It is big business, driven by marketing, and the client is the parent, not the child. Nurseries are advertised on television with bouncy music, good-looking staff and kids having fun. There is more serious editorializing too – professionals, we are told, will surround your child with stimulation and nurturing, probably beyond what you yourself could provide. You owe it to your child to give it this enriched, educational and socially developing environment. There is no time to lose! This is an especially potent message for the insecure young mother or father – as well as the highly competitive one!

While researching this book I talked to nursery-care staff in centres all over the world. Their honesty was often stunning – it was as if they had been waiting to tell someone the dark truth about what they really thought. One nursery director put it this way:

- 'It there was a fire, it would be my child I would rescue first.'

Others put it less graphically:

- 'I care about these kids, but I don't love them.'
- 'I care for them, but it does get on top of you after a while. Sometimes I hate them.'
- 'It's very stressful here, we have staff changing all the time.'
- 'I wouldn't have my own child here.'
- 'We do the best we can.'

Sometimes the childcarers were frankly angry at parents and their priorities:

- 'The mothers, some of them, they just don't care. They'd leave their kids here all the time if we let them.'
- 'I don't know why some of these parents have kids.'

In the early days of crèches and daycare centres, idealistic and caring people – usually older women with feminist principles – gave themselves wholeheartedly to providing a good environment. These centres were not very profitable, but they worked quite well because their staff *gave more to their roles than money could ever pay them.* Some were even volunteers. So caring, even loving, was possible, and long-term relationships were forged between mothers, children and carers. Also in those times, extremely young children were rarely cared for – except in emergencies, the children were at least two or three years old.

Today the money motive is much stronger in the nursery world, and this inevitably creates a tension. Consequently, savings are sometimes made through inadequate staffing, cost-cutting on resources. Governments try to prevent this by accreditation schemes and quality guidelines, but the result is often a kind of 'smoke and mirrors' game. In Australia recently, disgruntled employees of one large corporate chain told ABC Radio about a large van carrying extra play equipment, and extra staff, which would arrive at a centre a few days before a scheduled inspection. When the inspection was over, they would pack up the extra goodies, move on and things would go back to normal.

Taking shortcuts on staffing numbers, nappy supplies, food quality, crowding and cleaning, low pay for staff and using unqualified staff are all natural tendencies when profit is the driving force. Caring takes effort and it is often unrewarded, and so easily goes into decline. The consumers want childcare to be cheap, yet cheap and quality cannot go together. If it is quality, it is going to cost a lot. There is simply no way around this reality.

Do nurseries teach you to be social?

One of the claims made for nurseries is that they teach social interaction – and for three- and four-year-olds, this is certainly true. Yet it is clear from research that the under-threes do not play together successfully – they might fascinate each other for a few minutes, but they can only play successfully at this age with an adult or older child who 'scaffolds' the interaction, sensitively helping to make the game fun and easy. Another toddler may seem to adults like a potential playmate for our child, but as every parent of toddlers discovers, it just doesn't work out. Two toddlers playing together quickly become a source of either boredom or frustration to each other. We have all seen toddlers go from a moment of tender exploration, straight into mutual clobbering with a handy plastic toy. Left alone like this, they will only learn fear and aggression. In a nursery – a virtual toddler jungle – much of a carer's time is taken up preventing fighting and consoling the victims when they got there too late to prevent the fight.

The nanny option

Financially well-off parents in the UK often choose an alternative to the nursery option – they hire a nanny. This has two advantages: their child can stay at home, and receive 1:1 or 1:2 care. Theoretically, at least, this is a huge step forwards in terms of the quality of interaction their child will receive.

However, nannying raises a whole set of new issues, a topic of endless discussion wherever nanny users lunch together! Employing a nanny is a financial relationship, yet it is muddied with the intimacy of being part of your family. A nanny is in charge of the children, but subservient to you. Yet if the children are critical of her, you may have to criticize her on their behalf. You don't have to be a family therapist to see how tangled this can become.

There is a deeper danger too, felt at some level by all parents who use nannies – you could almost call it the Mary Poppins Syndrome. If a nanny does her job well, then your children will come to love her, and if she does it for long hours and more than a few months, they may come to love her more than they love you. The better a nanny is for your children, the more she will replace you. Is this really what you want?

An Australian lifestyle magazine recently interviewed a French couple who owned a famous winery. The couple explained how they brought out a new nanny from France each year to care for their children. They changed their nannies on an annual basis, they explained, '... in case the children got too attached to them'. How sad this sounds, given what we know about children's needs. What exactly was wrong with 'too attached'? Isn't that what life is all about? Would that be a reason for getting divorced – we were getting too attached to each other?

In spite of these hazards, a nanny arrangement can work well if you are extraordinarily lucky with your nanny, are able to share your children's affections, and can move beyond the commercial aspects to one of real trust and long-term involvement. Perhaps a little in moderation is a help, but family or friends, if available, are a much safer option for organizing your infants' supplementary care.

In a nutshell

- Nursery carers are hard pressed to offer real warmth and comfort to babies.
- Cortisol studies reveal the worrying effects of long-lasting stress on babies left in care.
- Nurseries are big business and the profit motive works against quality care.
- Nursery staff themselves feel unappreciated and critical of the system.
- The nanny option gives a baby or toddler much more individual care. But if overused it can introduce a whole new set of problems. And it's very expensive.

Part Three

Home and the World

Little children need to be with their parents. But the UK – with its soaring house prices, meagre government support, and an inflexible workplace culture, is destroying family life. How can couples win the freedom to raise their children with time and love? What has to change to help them? And what can they do in the meantime?

8

Couples at the coalface

Every family's situation is unique, but we can usually learn something from the stories of others, the choices they made and how they worked out.[1] A number of families were specially interviewed for this book, and three stories are related here in detail. All three of the couples here are sliders or 'adaptives', to use Catherine Hakim's term, since this is the group that has the greatest challenge of finding a balance. Their accounts show – with painful reality as well as admirable honesty – what works, what doesn't, and why.

1 Having it all?

First, let's meet the Bernacci family. Luke is an electrical fitter and Millie is a chemist. The Bernaccis started out with big plans, aiming to have four kids as well as both parents keeping on working full-time. They discovered that you *can* have it all – but only a bit at a time. Millie tells the story:

'When our first baby, Ben was born, I took four months' maternity leave, then did four months part-time, and then I went back to work full-time. Luke worked shifts and we shared the parenting, and at four months of age we put Ben with a childminder for three days a week.

'It was important to me to go back to work, and I'm very glad I did. I didn't want to lose my identity and it was nice to go where no one was crying, you could make a whole phone call without being interrupted, you could finish at the end of the day and think, "Ooh, I did that well." With childrearing, you finish at the end of the day and just have a list of everything you've done wrong. When you start being a parent it takes a long time to replace the recognition you get at work.

'There's no woman alive who doesn't spend the first week back at work in floods of tears. It's just the hardest thing. I had a fantastic childminder and she's now a very close friend, she taught me a lot about parenting that I would never have learned any other way. I loved being a mum and adore babies but I loved being back at work and feeling I could do both and I felt very capable and strong.

'Nursery wasn't what I really wanted. It's very difficult to find a good nursery and in my opinion the problem with nurseries is that you have a high turnover of staff and there's no consistency and the one thing that children really need is consistency. If you find a good childminder it's amazing as they have complete consistency.

'Two years later I had my second child. When I went back to work again it all became more complicated and difficult. You're running such a tight ship that if the slightest thing goes wrong – a train breaks down, etc. – I got immensely stressed. It took nothing to set the whole thing off.

'My little girl had troubles at the childminder because I didn't give her a bottle early enough and I was handing her over to the childminder later because I took a full six months of maternity leave this time. I expressed milk at work for her to have in the daytimes, but at the childminders she refused the bottle all day long and then she'd feed all night and it was a complete nightmare, and this went on for three months and she'd scream and cry all day at the childminder. One day I was so desperate to feed her before work I pushed the bottle in too hard and hurt her tongue.

'I knew I wanted a big family; at least three and probably four. I got pregnant with my third and it was quite difficult at that point. I had two children with the childminder and I was pregnant so I was very tired. Luke and I were very stressed. I just didn't see how you could work with three. I didn't want to give up my family, but I didn't want to give up my job. The problem was solved for me – I had a flat-out fight with my boss and handed in my notice the next day. As soon as I'd made the decision to leave I knew it was the right decision to make. I stopped feeling stressed immediately.

'I didn't know how I was going to support myself financially. We'd always had two incomes. We started living differently. We gave up our car and just shopped slightly differently and it really hasn't been too difficult. You're not spending money on clothes for work any more, you're not spending money on dry cleaning, not on transport, lunches, croissants, coffees and that's a significant hunk of your income. So it was very scary at the beginning, giving up my job as you're giving up your whole identity, your whole role. When you meet people on the street you say "Oh, I am ..." and it was very difficult to say, "Oh, I am a mother."

'It's much harder being at home but I very, very rarely wake up in the middle of the night feeling stress, and that used to happen the whole time. You're not juggling things in the same way. I never for one minute have wanted to be back at work.'

Being away from work wasn't easy for Millie – either psychologically or financially. But it was better than being torn in half like before. And with her characteristic energy, Millie began to find involvement in her community, and the time to enjoy it, and life started to make sense.

'The biggest difference is that you get involved in the local community. You hang around the school gates, you get to know people, you bump into people at the doctor's, you have coffees, you go to local classes with the kids, you get to meet different groups of people. You get involved with local politics sometimes, you campaign for local parks. And because you're not rushing all the time, you can chat to the shopkeepers, you can get to know people. And it's been overwhelming the difference to my life this has made. I've lived in this area 15 years and until I gave up work my local shopkeeper didn't know who I was, wouldn't let me off the 50 pence I was short of. And then I stopped work and had Mattie. I couldn't walk a minute in this area without having someone stop. I had to have half-hour conversations in every shop I went into. Everyone cuddled him, he had coins pressed into his palm. He was born into a completely different world than the others. And we're in a Sure Start area which is fabulous. It's made an enormous difference to the services. There's baby gym, there's singing lessons, there's yoga for mums with a crèche, swimming lessons, outings they put on – a lot of things going on.

'Now I feel proud of my life – I wanted to work and I did, but I changed when it became impossible. Now I am a parent full-time. One day I will go back to paid work. But for now this feels right for our family.'

2 The handbag decoy and the nursery from hell

Ella and Patrick McMillan have three children – Henry, eight, and twins Micah and Zoe, four. Ella is a journalist and Patrick a musician. In the beginning Ella and Patrick seemed to have a great set-up – a house in the country, complete with live-in carer. But the demands of career forced a move to the big city, and then it all started to go wrong. This story is memorable both for its chain of obstacles and for Ella's invention of the 'handbag decoy' technique for working in a newspaper office. The McMillans' story shows what terrible things the British workplace culture can do to young families. Ella tells the story:

'I tried every type of childcare arrangement before my son started school, and never found anything that worked perfectly. The live-in au pair when we lived in the country began as the most promising option, but she was unable to get up before 7 am when I needed to take the train from our country retreat to the office in London, and so I would park the baby outside her room in a car seat, push her door open and hope that when the baby cried, she would wake up. She had never started work before 11 am in her native Spain, she later explained. From what I could gather, on my return every night she rarely took the baby out but did seem to consume masses of telly, usually with the baby on her knee. She was extremely kind-hearted and happy, but fairly overweight, and when I asked why she hadn't gone for the walk, she would always reply, "Well, it looked like it was going to rain." I tried to explain that every day in England looked like it was going to rain.

'Moving to London to accommodate my husband's and my own job meant a squeeze on space, and we could only afford a tiny two-bedroom flat with no space for an au pair. By this time, baby Henry was 18 months old and had just qualified for the nearby nursery, "Busy Fingers", that took children at his age. However, the nursery shut at 6 pm, which meant leaving the office at 5 pm latest, when most of my colleagues on the newspaper never left before 6 pm or, more often, 7 pm. Presenteeism was a big factor in the swaggering, male-orientated atmosphere of the newspaper, and there was always a macho quality in leaving the work of the day to the last minute. My leaving early, despite getting in at 9 am when no one else arrived before 10 am, became a big source of snide remarks from colleagues. Surprisingly, other (mainly childless) women were among the least sympathetic. My boss used to make jokes like "thanks for popping in" when he saw me tidying my desk to leave.

'Eventually, we moved to a house and I found a more expensive nursery that was the only one in the area that was open until 7 pm. This gave me an extra hour to be present at the office, and on the appointment of a new boss, I consciously tried to distract attention away from my childcare difficulties. I brought in a spare jacket and handbag, and would leave the jacket over the back of my chair and put the handbag down by my feet when it was time to slip away, and always leave my computer on. Because being an editor required talking to other journalists, often on different floors, with my computer still winking in the corner, everyone assumed that I was around, but not at my desk.

'However, there were occasions when I would be stuck in a meeting, unable to slip out – and would miss the nursery deadline of 7 pm. On one occasion, I was pregnant with the twins and dashing across London in the car – phoning ahead to say that I would be a few minutes late. After being further delayed by an accident, I finally reached the nursery at 7.15 pm. I was met by two teenage girls waiting by the door, and watched in horror as my son slipped from between their legs to run *across the road* to greet me. The next day I got a bill for £70 from the nursery for two people having to wait 15 minutes. I paid £20, had a rude phone call from the twenty-something manager of the nursery about being late on more than one occasion, and immediately took my son out. I only wish I had reported them to the local authority for negligence at the same time.'

3 Living within your means

The Campbells, Danielle, 36 – mother and part-time IT consultant – and Zachary, 38 – father and civil engineer – have three daughters, now aged nine, six and four. The Campbells planned their finances so they could make it on one income when the time came. Danielle applied herself to parenthood with the same dedication she had applied in her career. She writes beautifully about how the investment of time in her daughters has paid off:

'I was probably unusual in that I always thought I would want to stay at home with our babies despite having a enjoyable and well-paid career. Consequently, when my husband and I bought our home we did not financially over-extend ourselves. I loved my job, and was a team leader of thirty people for five years. When I became pregnant with our first daughter, my managing director was not amused. We were a small company, which had been disrupted by four consecutive maternity leaves of fellow directors. I had been promoted on the understanding that I wasn't planning a baby. It was clear to me that the hours I was working and the travel that my job entailed were not compatible with my idea of motherhood. I had worked extremely hard for eight years, and I knew that I wanted to fully appreciate my baby. I expected a fair amount of mild censure from my colleagues regarding my decision to "stay at home". Some of the more senior women I worked with had been the first wave of successful women in my field of work. Surprisingly, no one was critical of my decision. One colleague in her fifties – a renowned feminist – told me that her one regret was not spending more time with her children while they were small. I also witnessed at first hand the trial of working motherhood through the experiences of some of my contemporaries – the concern when little children were ill, the irresponsibility of a rogue nanny, and the consuming guilt of leaving small babies in someone else's care. It didn't look appealing.

'My husband was supportive of my decision and took the view that it was for me to decide whether I wanted to return to work or not. I found the first year at home very hard, although I can only say this in retrospect since at the time I was determined not to question my decision. I adored my baby, and wanted to spend every minute with her. However, I desperately missed my job. I had loved the status, the financial independence, the intellectual demands of my former life. I also loved the social dynamics and the interesting people with whom I worked. My extended working hours during my pregnancy had meant I hadn't been involved in any ante-natal groups, and had it not been for one super friend, who had taken voluntary redundancy and had a baby the same age as mine, I would have been very lonely. As it was the days sometimes seemed rather long – daily walks to the park and the repetitive aspects of domestic life. Twenty months after our first baby was born, we had another daughter. By this stage my elder daughter was becoming really good company. I had made some good friendships with non-working mummies, the majority of whom were educated women with a similar outlook to myself. Not since university had I had such amount of time to be devoting to friendships. I also found having a toddler and a baby far more rewarding since the day was so busy and my own experience and confidence in my mothering ever growing.'

So, although it was tough adjusting, Danielle was patient and Zack was supportive of whichever choice she made. And then, when the time was just right, some work opportunities came along:

'At about this time, when my older daughter was two and our baby eight months, I was offered some consultancy work. I was really missing having some of my own money to spend. My husband would have liked to be more generous, however the restrictions of a single income had meant that there had been few new clothes, meals out, etc. A sharp contrast to our dual income life. I found that my "working confidence" had diminished, however I took the work, and really enjoyed it. During the following six years, and the arrival of my third daughter, I was able to juggle the work opportunities as they arose. My business has grown, and thanks to my first client's success, it has become a well-paid second career, which I have managed around the children. I have had very little childcare and have remained at home with our daughters; however, as they have become older, starting school and nurseries, I have been able to increase the work I do.

'There have been times when I have mildly resented my husband. His career has prospered and I have occasionally wondered what I would be doing had our roles been reversed. But I have always had an innate sense that there would come a time when I will once again be able to invest in my own career. Will I be a senior director? Probably not, but would I swap what I have with the restrictions of an office job – no matter how high-powered? I would not.

'What do I have? I have the most lovely relationship with my three little girls and a relaxed and happy marriage. I feel I know and appreciate my daughters to a degree that only spending enormous amounts of time together can guarantee. I feel that they are having the most secure, loving and fun childhood, which will make them well-rounded people. I try not to be too evangelical about "stay-at-home" mothers, because I do recognize that I am fortunate in finding a natural enjoyment of being with small children. I am not enormously patient generally, but for the girls I seem to find I am. Had I not become involved in this business, I feel I could have been fulfilled as a teacher. I love the fact that I have shaped my daughters' perceptions. They all have a high sense of justice and a sensitivity to other people's feelings. They are articulate, good company and kind. But the aspect I am most proud of is their tremendous friendship with each other. Perhaps I am just lucky with the compatibility of their natures, however I also feel that my mothering has contributed to their great friendship with each other. They have never had to fight for my attention, however the demands of a full-time mother with a small business means I expect them to play together and entertain themselves. Their friendship with each other gives us huge joy.

'I'd like to think I am also a good role model for their future working lives. I often tell them that the work I do from home enables me to treat the family to clothes, books and outings which we could otherwise not afford. They know I take pleasure from not only working but contributing to the family income. But I also hope to emphasize to them that perhaps achieving a balance in one's life is as important as smashing glass ceilings. I feel strongly that we should be encouraging our daughters to think ahead. I will encourage my daughters to pursue their own paths, however, if these paths are compatible with working part-time or from home, then so much the better.'

Making life complicated

Other correspondents described how they coped and were creative, or were battered down by bad luck, unsupportive employers, and the expense of living on one income.

The Hassans, Sandy and Dave, had a mother-in-law who was amazing – she travelled by train from Poole to London, took the baby home with her every Monday morning and returned her on the Tuesday night. Eventually, she moved to live closer so that the system would work better.

The Ruprechts, Liza and Iain, were halfway through maternity leave when Liza's employer – a women's magazine – called her in for a meeting. They demoted her from editor to writer, on two-thirds of her pay. Liza spent her maternity leave and first year back at work in a stressful and protracted legal battle, and eventually left in frustration.

The Danielsons, Hannah and Karl, simply collapsed under the stress of their combined jobs and trying to care for a second baby with sleeping problems. Hannah wrote:

'My doctor thinks I should be on medication for the stress. When I went in and she signed me off the first time it was really upsetting because I had both children on my knee and Leo was crying and Ellie, my three-year-old, was crying and saying, "Don't talk about work." The doctor just said, "You cannot talk about this in front of your children and you need to smile at your children more" – the kind of things that really make you feel guilty, and I felt really bad.

'I got very depleted, with Leo not sleeping much and a few postpartum health problems of my own, so that I didn't have the reserves to deal with it. Feeling very vulnerable, and then what was worse was being pitied by people at work, it was unbearable. And you start to sense that you're being pitied and devalued all over again because you're not going back to work and you're not wanted by your work. And I just found that really hard when you could see the look on people's faces, like, you're failing. I've always felt like I was really lucky and that I was a really positive person, and all of a sudden four or five categories of my life were really hard and you don't want to feel a burden on friends or feel like they don't want to call you because they'll have to listen to this diatribe.'

Hannah's situation is sad and dangerous, yet many UK women would echo her experience. The work–family issue has become a crisis of family mental health.

Where do the dads fit into all this?

Women make their choices in a context, and no one looms larger in this than the men they share their lives with. Often fathers interviewed for this book expressed a wish to share more in the care of their children, to work shorter hours or go part-time when their baby was born. Some had achieved this, while others found that their good intentions fell by the wayside.

Fathers affect the choices a mother has in surprising ways. Researchers were surprised to find that the length of time a mother chose to breastfeed was determined most strongly by the *husband's* attitude. This finding has lead to researchers paying much more attention to how powerfully a father affects his children, not only directly but also via the support he gives to his wife in her mothering role. Fathers can make or break a mother's efforts to raise her child well. A husband who is less in touch with a baby's needs might see the mother's role as less important, and lean on her to return early to work. Another might prefer her to be at home, and discourage her from returning to a career she enjoys and is good at. Women have minds of their own, but it is easier to decide freely when partners are generally supportive.

Each couple needs to negotiate a tailor-made arrangement that suits their own unique needs. The trick is to make it fair – so there is no chance for resentments to accumulate. The pleasures and the pain of parenthood can be shared if people are willing to wait their turn. Encouragingly, around 1 in 15 fathers now spend time as the stay-home parent – it is hardly a majority, but the proportion is growing. Things seems to work far better if the mother can stay at home for the first year, when she is simply more equipped by nature to be the primary carer, and the mother-child bond is being established. But thereafter, fathers may be as good a carer – or even better – if they are motivated and the mother is keen to return to her paid job. Many couples we spoke to had an agreement that involved some exchanging of roles, and this has to be a good thing. The era of the distant, disengaged father, damaging for kids and sad for fathers too, is thankfully coming to an end.

In a Nutshell

- A wide range of families interviewed show that you can't have it all. At least not all at once.
- Families who live more simply win back the freedom of how to use their time.
- Fathers who are willing to share parenting of young children are part of the solution.

Our world of greed
and speed

Most people today consider themselves to be free. They feel that they can decide for themselves – from the smallest things in life to the biggest: what to eat for lunch, what clothes to buy, where to live, what job to do, whether or not to have children, and how to raise them. The option to stay at home when your children are very young, or return to paid work should be a freely-made choice. But it is here that you begin to wonder if your life is really as free as you believe.

None of us lives our life in a vacuum – there are social pressures, financial necessities, attitudes and expectations of family and friends. On top of this are the economic manipulations of governments and employers, and the whole circus of the mass media telling us how we should live. All of this can combine to make you feel there is no other way than a life of non-stop work. Yet there is always some room for choice; like a swimmer in a river, if you are aware of the currents, you can swim with them, against them, across them, or decide this river is not for you!

Life has changed a great deal in just two generations. Had a person fallen asleep 50 years ago, and then woken up in the present, they would be astounded at the changes. At first it might seem wonderful – mobile phones, cheap air travel, antibiotics, flat-screen TV and so on – but soon they would notice some things that were less enjoyable, and the speed and pressure of life would be at the heart of these. People today are healthier, richer, but they are not as close or even as happy as they were in an earlier era.

We often hear the word 'globalization' and think it has something to do with big business and international trade. We rarely realize its implications for every single person on the planet. Sometime in the last ten years, a handful of shy, brown people wandered out of a rainforest somewhere, and were given some trinkets. The last human beings on earth had finally been incorporated into the global economy. Communism has gone, capitalism has triumphed, and we don't know how to steer it or slow it down. In the world defined by corporate values and ways of living, only two activities really matter – *earning and spending*. Only these activities seem to earn respect, and make you feel included and worthwhile; tragically they have become the central pillars of our society. All those other aspects of life which can't be measured in pounds and pence now don't really count and are pushed aside: such things as friendship, peace of mind, kindness, love, creativity, nature, laughter, spirituality and joy cannot easily be put in a box and bought or sold, so they drop out of sight.

There is a further, perhaps worse consequence of the 'earn and spend' life. Not only are 'unproductive' activities (such as watching a sunset at the beach, or chatting to a neighbour) disappearing, but certain kinds of people are disappearing from view as well. The very old and very young, the disabled, the slow and the sick, the mentally different, have no value in the world of earn and spend. They are inconveniences to be managed. They are hidden away in specialized institutions, pushed to the edges of society out of sight. Nothing must get in the way of productivity.

All of this affects you too. If you are not engaged in the business of earning and spending – for instance if you decide, as a father or mother, to stay at home for a time and care for your child – it is likely you may feel rather lost. A bit useless and devalued. This situation is terribly inhuman and unsustainable – it takes the most vital and meaningful parts of our lives and degrades them. Our children may grow up thinking that possessions are the heart of life. We ourselves feel empty, drained and unsatisfied. Something has to be done. Our greatest weapon is choice, based on a personal idea of values – of what matters most, and so I want to make a values statement here that is clear and explicit:

There is nothing more important in this life
than the relationships we make
with other human beings.

If you agree with this, then it provides a yardstick and a compass for every minute of your life. While the world around us gives us, relentlessly, a thousand times a day, the toxic and bizarre message: 'You are what you own', let me suggest a different ethos, a different way of measuring human worth and identity: 'We are who we love.' Family, community, friendship and love matter so much more than anything we might ever own and spend. They also bring more happiness. Relationships create us, nurture us, develop us and define us, and the most important and long-lasting of all our relationships is the one we have with our babies and children.

Most people would rush to agree with this – it is often said by politicians – but the problem is that the rhetoric is at odds with how we are driven to live. The reality is that we live more and more alone. We watch *Neighbours* on TV instead of talking to our real neighbours. We have enormous trouble keeping our marriages together. Vast numbers of people of all ages now live alone. Extended families rarely get together. Old people are far away, virtually imprisoned, in retirement ghettos and nursing homes. We have given up on people, except at the lowest level – in casual friendships and easily interchangeable social events. We buy music instead of making music. We substitute shopping for socializing, TV for talking, food for sex, and we wonder why we feel so unsatisfied.

We *can* choose

We are not all helpless victims though; our own choices play a part in this too – such as the idea that we 'must have' beautiful homes, overseas holidays, plasma screen TVs, more clothes than we have room for in our wardrobes. Many young couples feel that they must own all these things as soon as they are old enough to leave home. We are put under pressure, but we also must shoulder some of the blame. We can trap ourselves, through not stopping to think what is really important. In racing to 'have it all' something has to give. Young couples who are caught up with material goals tend to delay having children, then have them on the last tick of their biological clocks, while not wanting to compromise busy careers or expensive lifestyles. If we are too greedy, it affects others with less choice. The soaring cost of housing arising from all this new disposable income means that less affluent families have to work longer hours to survive.

The big choice for us all today is a choice between love and money. This choice will manifest in a thousand different ways throughout your lifetime, but essentially it will always boil down to the same issue. We all need money, but there is a difference between needing it and being ruled by it. It is all about the order in which you put things. The trick with life is setting priorities, or they will set you.

If you put love first, and the people you love first, then every little decision is changed. You will soon come to realize that hurry, the sense that there isn't enough time and things must be done quickly and without delay, is the enemy of love. If you choose to put love first, then your life will slow down. Material things – since they cost time, and take you away from your family – may come to mean less. Community – since it provides your needs in a different way to what can be bought – may become more important. You begin to find better community, less dependency on money, more involvement with others. You start to feel that your life has soul.

This book cannot tell you how to live your life. But there is one thing it can promise: when love becomes the guiding principle of your life, then everything changes. You will not regret it.

In a nursing home on the outskirts of the city, an old woman is living out her last hours. Her eyes are closed and every breath she takes is an effort. All of a sudden, she rouses and calls out in an alarmed, high-pitched voice. A cleaner, the only person about at this late hour, hears her from the corridor, comes in and takes the old woman's hand. The old woman is saying something, but the cleaner does not understand what. A few moments pass and then the old woman's grip eases and her breathing stops. The cleaner sighs and goes to tell the matron. The old woman's grown-up children are miles away; they will come tomorrow to sort out the paperwork.

In a nursery in the middle of the city, a baby is lying in a cot. She is wide awake, her eyes dart about brightly and her arms wave. She seems to frown, carefully and intently her lips form to shape a word, and she speaks it out loud. A childcare attendant smiles momentarily, glances her way, then turns away to attend to a crying child nearby. She doesn't know it is the baby's first spoken word.

It is an odd time we live in, a scary time when intimacy is being outsourced and caring is purchased from strangers. We have never in history lived such isolated lives. Where once we lived our whole lifespan within walking distance of the people near and dear to us, today we are lucky if we can even keep a family of three or four together.

The concept of self-sacrifice, of putting someone else first for a time, has almost disappeared. Yet this is at the heart of what love means – especially when love is between a self-reliant adult and a totally dependent child. We have all known of too much sacrifice – of mothers in the 1950s whose intelligence and creativity was wasted by the limitations on their roles; of fathers who worked themselves into early graves because they thought being a 100-per cent provider was the only role for a man. But self-sacrifice is not the malaise of the twenty-first century for we have taken self-indulgence to dizzying heights. Our teenagers are often more moral and more socially concerned than we are, but they are also more depressed, more distrustful, more adrift. We haven't done our job. We haven't kept alive the social network of caring people amongst which they can take their place. Now there is only the shopping mall and the nightclub. They look to their peer group for comfort, wisdom and meaning, but find only other lost souls.

This book is not arguing for a return to the past, but rather that we reconsider what is precious in our own humanity. A new viewpoint is emerging, that there is a middle road, that life is long enough to fulfil ourselves, and also to give some years of our life to young children. Having children brings joy in proportion to what we invest in them – the best things in life are often hard-earned, and one of these is seeing young adults who love us and enjoy being with us, who we have set on the road with our care and, yes, even our sacrifice. We can preserve a sense of self, in fact we can enhance our sense of self, by devoting part of our life to others.

The biggest lie, the biggest deception of popular culture is the infantile notion that we can have it all. We can't – everything has a price. Wealth almost always comes at a cost to family wellbeing. Hurry erodes love. Self-centredness costs us in the loneliness it leaves behind, in the relationships we neglected to build because building them involved giving them our time. The lesson of all this is a tough one – we have to choose. We have to prioritize things. We have to let some things go. We have to give something up to get something more precious.

Selfishness is a stage of life. It is the most natural feature of childhood, and transcending it is the clearest marker of a mature human being. Being able to put oneself second – just for a time – is at the heart of parenthood. The arrival of a totally dependent baby catapults us into a self-or-other dilemma of life-shattering proportions.

Are children in trouble?

The rapid uptake of nursery care in the early years has been a huge social experiment; it is essentially a gamble taken by millions of parents that 'everything will be okay'. The results of that experiment are now emerging. The first generation of babies raised in nursery care are now entering their teens and early twenties. There are few if any studies of this generation which differentiate the nursery-reared from the home-reared young people, or the large group who are some combination of the two. What we do know is that this whole generation is in crisis.[1] Most Western industrial countries are reporting record levels of young people with mental health problems, most notably suicide and depression. (Suicide by young males has increased fourfold in the Western world in the last 30 years.) The proportion of teenagers in the UK with behaviour problems has doubled since 1980, the proportion with anxiety and depression has risen by 70 per cent. Across Britain, 24,000 teenagers a year are admitted to hospital following suicide attempts. The charity Childline has noted a rise in self harm of 65 per cent in just the last two years.[2, 3]

The incidence of attention problems, violence problems, eating disorders, binge drinking and other addictions has also risen dramatically. There is now a widespread concern among health officials about the use of anti-depressant drugs for children, and in some classrooms one in five kids are prescribed Ritalin or a similar amphetamine-based stimulant to manage problem behaviour.

These are not the poverty-stricken children of an earlier time, lacking education, healthcare or food; affluent children are equally represented in this problem generation. Within mental health, law enforcement and youth work agencies, alarm bells are ringing with regard to how children are shaping up. What is more, when these children reach adulthood their problems seem to compound. Demographers have noticed a growing failure among young adults to form close relationships and make them last. More than half of all marriages end (the median length of these marriages is about eight years). Increasing numbers of young couples opt not to have children, thereby missing out on potentially the most important relationship(s) of their life. Many of today's young adults will either delay committing to long-term relationships until their mid-thirties, or not commit at all. The fastest-growing household type in the UK is single people living alone.[4]

We don't know if day nurseries have played a part in these changes: no one has thought to study these correlations. What we do know is that lack of parental time and weaker relationships with parents are a critical factor in all of these problem areas – from suicide to drug abuse, problems with the law to teen pregnancy. There is a strong consensus among professionals that the unprecedented epidemic of mental health problems in the young is due to the hurried and disconnected way that families now live their lives.[5] Parents don't set out to be worse or less caring parents than those of earlier generations – far from it. The problem is in the way that we live. There are impossible stresses that our economic system puts on mothers and fathers, and in particular the terrible choice they must make between career or family. People do not have enough time to parent their children properly.

The nursery care question is part of a bigger problem of a society that has lost its sense of values – of what really matters. For many people, life has become an express train of uncertain destination. We are hurrying, but we don't really know where to. Children and adolescents are like corks that bob on the waves of the adults' stresses and strains: they are the first to show the symptoms of a sick culture. And they are now showing them in epidemic proportions.

The childcare debate is one of the most emotionally intense topics of contemporary society. Controversies that go this close to people's hearts generate a lot of emotion, so it is most important to separate fact from fiction, and clear thinking from ideology. This book does not take an ideological position, either fundamentalist right, or simplistic left. It is definitely not an argument to go back to a past of women alone at home with kids while men slave away at work. A completely new arrangement of our lives is needed; we need to develop ways of living a more enriched life that are not built on ever-escalating material desire.

Where our children fit in

It's no surprise that children don't fit in well to this modern arms-length world. The wonderful movie *About A Boy* illustrates this very well. The anti-hero played by Hugh Grant is the ultimate consumer; he is too rich to need to work, and surrounds himself with toys and expensive distractions. He is intensely irritated by the sheer inconvenience of a real child arriving in his life, along with a mentally-ill mother who promptly attempts suicide! The whole plot involves him discovering a deeper satisfaction that can only come from people – however much they complicate your life. Children *are* inconvenient, messy; they take time, they don't work on a schedule. Money won't fix what is wrong with them.[6] Like playing an instrument, tending a garden or learning to paint, raising children takes years of practice to do well. Yet at the same time they are such a huge plus in the lives of the people who love them. And, as the one in five couples who struggle with infertility will testify, they are also an extraordinary privilege.

No one will ever have as much effect on us, or be affected as much by us, as the children we raise. They often touch us more deeply even than our husband, wife or partner does. When we die, a few friends will remember us, but our kids' happiness and contribution to the world will be the direct result of our efforts. We will live on vividly and actively in their memories, and be a big part of what they in turn pass on to their children. Life will rarely give us such a huge opportunity to mess things up! Or such an opportunity for fun, joy and pride.

In a nutshell

- Earning and spending have become more important in our world than caring and communicating with those around us. Today's world runs on greed and speed.
- Childhood has changed, with much less time available and less sense of family or community. The heavy use of day nurseries for very young children is just one symptom of this.
- Your big decisions in life are between money and love. If you put love first, it changes everything.

10

A world where love can thrive

Nursery care is a great thing when used well. It's a matter of balance, of getting the timing right. The bulk of the research I have examined here indicates that in the first three years of life children are too vulnerable, too much in need of intimate care and all it can offer, to be left to group care by strangers.

So how can we better support parents who want to use nursery care in a more appropriate way than 'too early, too much, and for too long'?

Solutions – 'the big three'

In those European countries which have better support for families, today's generation of young parents do not have to choose the nursery care option for babies and toddlers, but can have what we could call the 'big three' necessary for families:

1. Paid parental leave;
2. Flexible work hours;
3. Guaranteed return to work.

These three conditions are what parents need, since they allow them to sequence their lives properly. In the UK, we have a long way to go in providing these basic needs.

Sweden is the best example of this – with probably the world's best quality nursery care available for all, usage for the under-threes has been *falling solidly for the last decade*.[1] Across continental Europe, parents are demanding – and getting – better alternatives to help them balance work and parenthood. The UK and the US lag behind seriously in these areas, but I hope this book will help to remedy this state of affairs.

The role of politicians

Sue Gerhardt, in her excellent book *Why Love Matters*,[2] put it like this:

'At a wider social level, I believe that the real source of many parenting difficulties is the separation of work and home, of public and private, which has had the result of isolating mothers in their homes, without strong networks of adult support and without variety in their daily routines. These conditions create much of the depression and resentment that are so problematic for baby's devel-opment. Women face the artificial choice of devoting

themselves to their working life or to their babies, when
the evidence is that they want both.'

Politicians must now begin to create the conditions that
families can thrive in – extended parental leave, flexible working hours and a guaranteed return to work are most prominent among these. A plunging birth rate will probably
succeed in forcing their hand where years of lobbying has
failed. The family-friendly policies already adopted in France
and Scandinavia show the way, and sure enough, in these
countries, young couples are once again starting to have children a little younger and more often.

Be the change you want to see

Governments, of course, play a major role in how society
deals with these issues, but we cannot leave this all to governments. Instead we have to make changes and do some growing up ourselves to put this right. There is a part to be played
simply by living with less, in order to have wealth of a different kind – love, connection, community and time.
Thankfully, many young parents increasingly seem to be
becoming aware of this. They want a more balanced life than
their exhausted, stressed parents. In fact, we, the older generation, might have done them a good turn by showing them
how *not* to live a good life!

Quietly, change is coming around the world – people want
to raise their own children, not have someone else do it for

them. Home care of young babies puts people back in charge of their lives – it makes us less of a consumer and more of a person. Like eating organic food, walking for exercise (instead of paying a personal trainer to boot-camp us around the gym) and caring actively about world justice, it is part of a larger cultural shift – a turning away from the mass market, throw-away culture, and towards being self-reliant, sustainable, aware, empowered, liberated or, to use an old-fashioned term, wise.

Improving nursery care

The nursery-care industry has many good people working in it. Often they are aware of the problems and contradictions in their work, and constantly strive to make care as good as possible. Nurseries have been responsive to criticisms that I and other child development experts have made in the last ten years, and improvements have been significant.

Some centres keep children with their siblings to retain a family feeling. Some increase staff ratios beyond what government requires. Some centres pay their staff better rates so that they can remain in the job long-term and be steady presences in children's lives. More centres take time to liaise with parents, and help babies to settle in gradually to being cared for by someone new. Some even allocate babies a single primary carer, who can bond with them and make them feel more secure. Some centres are giving children better food and a quieter, less stressful environment. Some even actively discourage parents enrolling children younger than two.

It is possible to keep improving daycare indefinitely, but the expense is astronomical. The kind of love that a parent gives, were it to be measured in monetary terms, would be worth millions of pounds per child. The nursery care industry depends utterly on a supply of low-paid labour. *If nursery care workers were paid what they deserve, the industry would collapse.*

The strong feeling among European countries is that it is more cost-effective to subsidize parents of young children under the age of two to stay at home, than to subsidize nurseries which at best do a second-rate job of caring for this age group.

The nursery nightmare is not over yet. Every year more and more parents put younger and younger babies into nurseries. There are nurseries in high buildings where children never touch the ground, and others where they never go outside and breathe fresh air. In some countries there are all-week crèches where children live round-the-clock, like baby boarding schools. Perhaps one day it will be possible simply to hand over one's newborn baby and check their progress on the internet. Virtual parenthood.

There is no doubt that parents need help. Penelope Leach[3] recommends a different kind of facility altogether – a family centre, present in every neighbourhood or suburb, where there can be found other parents to talk to, healthcare, sociable eating facilities, specialized parenting help, play equipment on loan, and someone to talk to about a developmental worry such as eye testing or co-ordination problems. These facilities would be modest in size and within walking distance of your home. You would get to know the staff – even volunteer there yourself – and meet and make friends with other parents.

This kind of facility would alter the whole lifestyle of the community around it. They already exist in some places, and work well – we just need more. The question we have to keep asking is, what do parents really need to do the best job they can with minimum stress and maximum richness of opportunity. Then keep going until we get there!

Given the evidence I have gathered as I travel the globe and meet young parents, I am full of hope that we will move on from these rather sad times we live in. The future will have nurseries and childcare centres available for all, but they will be used in a balanced way, and only rarely for the under-twos and sparingly for the under-threes. There will be no waiting lists for nursery places. The raising of very young children in large, commercial nurseries, with their emotionally sterile environments, plastic surfaces and bored, underpaid, undertrained and exhausted staff, will be looked on as a brief and horrible era, along with all the other nightmares of our child-rearing history – gin in the baby's bottle, child labour in the coal mines, and boarding school for six-year-olds. It will be, to quote a beautiful phrase, consigned to the dustbin of history. We will then have taken a significant step towards creating a world where love can truly thrive.

In a nutshell

- There has been a huge growth – a trebling in 20 years – in the number of children under three years old in full-time daycare.
- An epidemic of mental health problems has taken place among children and adolescents in that same span of time.
- The cause seems to lie in the whole lifestyle of hurry and stress, leading to a loss of family time, of which daycare of babies and toddlers is just a part.
- Parents in countries more advanced than the UK have begun to abandon the use of daycare, preferring the 'big three' – parental leave, flexible work hours, and return-to-work security.
- Revaluing time with our children is part of a growing sentiment among young parents. The tide is beginning to turn.

APPENDIX

Recommendations

The message of this book is simple:

The choices we make about childcare should be based on the developmental needs of our child.

Allowing for individual differences, my recommendations are as follows:

By age

In your child's first year

Do not use nursery care at all. Organize for your baby to be with a parent or grandparent all the time, except for occasional breaks – days off or evenings out – when you have a trusted and familiar babysitter.

When your child is one

Up to one short day per week, for example, 9 am to 3 pm, with a trusted and familiar carer. Ideally 1:1, but in a 1:3 ratio at the very most.

When your child is two

Up to two short days per week with a trusted and familiar carer. After two-and-a-half, a group setting like a good-quality nursery can be suitable for girls, but usually boys are not ready until three. Only use group care if the child settles well, and for half-days only. Some children are not ready until three or more, and group care can be upsetting and harmful for these children.

When your child is three

Up to three short days or half-days a week in a good-quality nursery or pre-school.

When your child is four

Up to four short days or half-days a week in a good-quality nursery or pre-school.

By type of care

In order of preference, the best source of childcare for your child *under the age of three*, if you are not able to care for them yourself, is:

1. *A close relative or friend* whom you trust and who loves your child.
2. *A trustworthy and friendly family day carer,* whom you know personally (see note below).
3. *A quality childcare centre,* with stable staff whom you get to know and feel comfortable with.

(Note: if you cannot find a family day carer you are totally comfortable with, then a nursery is probably better, because of the accountability that goes with an organized centre.)

For children three years and older, good childcare centres can come into their own. At this age, the benefits of social interaction, planned activities, playing space and equipment, and professionally trained and motivated staff are a major bonus.

By your circumstances

As well as the needs of the child, the needs of the family unit must be weighed in – because the child will suffer anyway if, for instance, a parent becomes sick, or a marriage breaks down, or a family cannot keep its home through lack of income. If childcare is truly good for your family, it will meet the following criteria:

1. It helps your survival – for instance, when you need to work to feed and house your family.
2. It gives you time to care adequately for other children, for example a new baby or a sick child.
3. It provides things for your child that you can't provide – resources (if poor), stimulation (if limited at home), friends (if isolated or an only child).
4. It meets your standards on discipline, respect for the child's being, and safety.
5. It builds long-term relationships – carers become your friends, and friends of your child.
6. It is a setting where you feel welcome to drop in at any time, spend the day with your child, make special requests or let them know of concerns without ever feeling you are a bother.

By balancing a child's needs, and your changing family situation, informed choices can be made which may work out very well.

Good luck!

Inside Stories

When *Raising Babies* was released we also opened a comments section on the www.stevebiddulph.com website. To our surprise, many comments came from nursery staff and directors, and others working in the childcare field. Here is a selection:

I totally agree with Steve Biddulph. I do have strong views about babies in nurseries – babies need their parents. I am an NVQ assessor and early years tutor. I teach my students about attachment, bonding and how the first few years of a child's life are so important. Some nurseries are very good but they can never meet the individual needs of very young babies like their parents can. Some nurseries are appalling. I have seen young children given a cup of soup, half a crumpet or a piece of cake for tea.

I personally think if a parent has to work they should use the child's grandparents or a recommended child-minder who would be prepared to mind their child with only one older child instead of putting a baby in a nursery where sometimes the ratio of babies to carers is a lot more than the 1 to 3 it should be. One to 3 is terrible – trying to feed three babies at a time is impossible, unhygienic and unfair.

I am a nursery teacher who studied in the early 1970s. Everything I was reading then, including a Government document on early education before five, warned of the developmental consequences for babies in nurseries. The regimentation as opposed to routine, the 'keep them fed, watered and dry' as opposed to loved, cuddled and close, led practitioners to question what benefit babies in nurseries were experiencing.

But nurseries are now big business and money makers for owners who often have no qualification or interest in child development. Parents beware. Seek out a good childminder, preferably one who comes with personal recommendation.

I have worked in various daycare settings for over 15 years and have seen what this kind of care does to young children. I can only bear to work with the over-threes now as my conscience will no longer allow me to keep quiet when prospective parents visit and ask for reassurance from me over their decision to put their three-, six- or eight-month-old baby into full-time daycare!

I often think it's ironic that people accept that older children need school holidays, half terms, etc., and yet they think nothing of putting under-fives in nurseries that open from 8 am to 6 pm for most of the year. I really think there should be some form of legislation to limit how many hours children spend in such places.

I have been in the field of early years education for 10 years. I truly believe that no matter how much you try to comply with OFSTED rules and regulations on care and educational standards for the little ones no one can give more love, cuddles and better listening skills than the parents themselves. We should educate the parents by being honest and making them aware of their positive contribution to their child's happiness which nurseries cannot offer at such an early age. Ratio alone does not allow it! Social interaction is a marketing tool used by all nursery chains to keep their register at full capacity!

I am a nursery nurse and I enjoy working with children but through the years I have felt very sorry for babies and toddlers who are left in nursery for long periods of time. So through what I have observed, I agree with all your findings in your research and applaud them. Even though I do recognize that a lot of parents do not want to accept the harsh reality of leaving their children at nursery, it is important that they come to terms with the negative side of long-term childcare if there's an imbalance. I personally think that the Government should enforce a policy where children under three should not exceed a certain amount of hours in nursery due to the detriment in their development.

I used to be a nanny and have temped in nurseries. I was shocked by the apathy and attitude of the staff at each nursery. Most of the staff didn't have a clue or just didn't care about the love and support and stimulation that these children needed. They were also paid a very low salary and all talked of moving on to somewhere else that could offer them more money. Yet when the parents arrived to collect their children the staff were suddenly full of how the children had had a wonderful day.

I live in one of the most affluent areas of the UK and know for a fact that the 'care' offered in many of the nurseries here is bordering on neglect. I find that parents often seem to be dazzled by local (very expensive) nurseries and do not even consider using a registered childminder. I think this is very sad as I know that there are many committed registered childminders out there offering a quality service where the children have the opportunity to only ever have one 'key worker' from birth up until they start school and beyond.

I would never, never, never expose either of my children to the daily 'life' in a day nursery and agree with everything that Steve has said with regard to under-threes in nurseries.

I have been running my nursery for 14 years and in that time have had one child who I feel managed to survive a 50-hour week without behaviour issues! I actively discourage parents from using us for full-time care because it certainly does not work for children. Working time regulations mean that adults cannot work more than 48 hours, so how can it be right for children!

Consequently I only have two children who are full time. I also do not take babies for similar reasons.

What this Government is advocating in the extended day will be so detrimental to our children and therefore society as a whole. There are so many contradictions in Government policies at the moment, as on the one hand a document states that they value the family, and the next one advocates the child being out of the family home for 50 hours a week. They state that children's health and behaviour will be improved yet just my experience shows the opposite happens.

As a former nursery manager for Barnardos and now a lecturer in childcare I have huge concerns on what we subject vulnerable and needy new human beings to when we place them in day nurseries.

I know the pressures of being a working parent and returned to full-time, demanding work when my daughter was 9 months, but hunted high and low for a wonderful childminder so that she would continue to have the stability and security of a known and capable adult that she learned to love and trust – vital elements for children to develop socially and emotionally. My wish would be that the Government truly recognized the value of parenting and raised its status above the level of 'scrounger'.

I am an early childhood teacher at a primary school in a low socioeconomic area of our town. What you are describing in your book is what I have observed and been calling 'childcare syndrome' for years. My colleagues and myself (for that matter every school) are witnessing and having to deal with the results of this phenomenon.

The main issue observed and of concern is (generally) poor oral literacy (in Grade 1) which leads to all forms of literacy and numeracy problems. This also can lead to other issues that were mentioned like behavioural problems and aggression, which is a huge concern for everyone at the school. Other observable characteristics of many of these children are, as mentioned, behavioural problems and attitudes such as 'some-one will clean-up after me' and 'I don't have to do that if I don't want to!'

I have been researching this with our behavioural management department's data and the numbers appear to reflect the observations noted above.

Notes

Introduction

1. Perhaps the first real warning sign was the switch in position by a previously strong supporter of daycare, Professor Jay Belsky, in his 1986 paper:

    Jay Belsky, 'Infant Daycare: a cause for concern?', *Zero to Three*, September 1986, pp 1–7

2. By 2003 this trickle had turned to an avalanche, with the release of NICHD's long-term study results:

    NICHD (National Institute of Child Health and Development), 'Does amount of time spent in child care predict socioemotional adjustment during the transition to kindergarten?', *Child Development*, 2003, 74, 976–1005

3. This was the title of Madeleine Bunting's book on the UK's extraordinarily long working hours, compared to other OECD countries. It is probably the most important text in this whole debate since it paints a grim picture of

a country manipulated and stressed by employers and government policies, so that family life is impaired and damaged, sometimes beyond repair.

M Bunting, *Willing Slaves: How the Overwork Culture is Ruling Our Lives*, HarperCollins, London, 2004

4. 'Although use of formal daycare is well established in Sweden, in practice its use is concentrated on children aged between three and seven years old.'

Pam Meadows, *Women at Work in Britain and Sweden*, National Institute of Economic and Social Research, London, 2000

'In Sweden, for example, it is unusual for children under eighteen months to be in public childcare.'

Irene Wolcott and Helen Glazer, *Work and Family Life: achieving integration*, Australian Institute of Family Studies, Melbourne, 1995

5. NICHD study data has been released progressively since 1991, most recently in 2005. A good example would be the 2001 below, which reports 'the findings did not merely reflect the fact that the children who spent more time in care were simply more assertive ... they were also more disobedient and defiant and aggressive and destructive.'

NICHD Early Child Care Research Network, 'Child care and children's peer interaction at 24 and 36 months', *Child Development*, 2001, 72 (5), 1478–1500

6. The UK EPPE study, with an equally large-scale follow-up of children, found similar results.

   Kathy Sylva, Edward Melhuish, Pam Sammons and Iram Siraj-Blatchford, *Effective Provision of Pre-school Education*, Institute of Education, London, 2004

7. A N Schore, 'Introduction and Effects of a Secure Attachment Relationship on Right Brain development, Affect Regulation, and Infant Mental Health', *Infant Mental Health Journal*, 2001, 22, 1–2

Chapter 1 – What nursery is like

1. Y Roberts, 'An adult approach to childcare', *Guardian*, 6 October 2005

2. Fiona Steele, 'To Improve Nurseries, we must improve conditions for nursery nurses', *Guardian*, 14 August 2004

3. Rosemary Murphy, quoted in M Bunting, 'Nursery Tales, Part Two', *Guardian*, 8 July 2004

Chapter 2 – Slammers and sliders

1. Patricia Morgan, 'Who Needs Parents: The Effects of Childcare and Early Education on Children in Britain and the USA', *Choice in Welfare Series No 31*, Institute of Economic Affairs, London, 1996

2. L G Russek and G E Schwartz, 'Feelings of parental caring predict health status in midlife: a 35-year follow-up of the Harvard Mastery of Stress Study', *Journal of Behavioural Medicine*, [date?], vol. 20, pp 1–13

3. Bunting, *Willing Slaves*.

4. Hakim, Catherine, *Work-Lifestyle Choices in the 21st Century: Preference Theory*, Oxford University Press, 2000

Chapter 3 – Does nursery school harm under-threes?

1. Bowlby's own classic is *Attachment and Loss* (3 vols), Penguin Books, New York, 1971–81.

A great overall summary of the work of Bowlby and Winnicott, the pioneering British researchers into child psychiatry and attachment, is written by Bowlby's son, Richard:

R Bowlby, *Fifty Years of Attachment Theory: Recollections of Donald Winnicott and John Bowlby*, Karnac Books, UK, 2004

2. Jay Belsky and M Rovine, 'Non-maternal care in the first year of life and the security of infant-parent attachment', *Child Development*, 1988, 59, 157–67; Jay Belsky, 'Infant Daycare: a cause for concern?'

3. NICHD, 'Does amount of time spent in child care predict socioemotional adjustment during the transition to kindergarten?'; NICHD Early Childcare Research Network, 'Child Care Effect Sizes', *American Psychologist*, November 2005

4. Clarke-Stewart, Alison, 'The "effects" of infant daycare reconsidered', *Early Childhood Research Quarterly*, 1988, 3 (3), 293–318.

5. A typical paper from among the dozens released using the NICHD data would be:

NICHD Early Childcare Research Network, 'Early childcare and self control, compliance, and problem behaviour at 24 and 36 months', *Child Development*, 1998, 69, 1145–70

An accessible summary in book form of the entire long-term study was published in February 2006:

NICHD (ed), *Childcare and Child Development*, Guildford Press, 2006

6. The UK press carried extensive coverage of the negative findings in 2004, and noted their growing impact on government policies. The findings and the support they gained from childcare professionals in the UK such as Drs Melhuish and Leach successfully influenced government thinking on parental leave.

   M Bunting, 'Fear on nursery care forces rethink', *Guardian*, 8 July, 2004

   M Bunting, 'Nursery Tales', *Guardian*, 8 and 9 July, 2004

7. Kathy Sylva, Edward Melhuish, Pam Sammons and Iram Siraj-Blatchford, *Effective Provision of Pre-school Education*

8. The Leach, Sylva and Stein study results were first released in a speech by Dr Leach to the National Childminding Association. Reported with comments in:

   Yvonne Roberts, 'Official: Babies do best with mother', *Observer*, 2 October 2005

9. Alison Clarke-Stewart, *Daycare – The Developing Child*, Fontana, Glasgow, 1982

10. Kay Margetts, 'Responsive caregiving, reducing stress in infant toddler care', *International Journal of Early Childhood*, 2005, 32, 2, 77–84

11. Cited in Anne Manne's powerful book on the daycare debate. Manne also gives insights into the politics of the NICHD study and the internal wrangles between the team, which likely meant that, if anything, its cautions were underplayed in its reports.

    A Manne, *Motherhood: How should we care for our children? Moving beyond the Mother Wars*, Allen and Unwin, Sydney, 2005

12. M Bunting, 'Nursery Tales'

13. Australian academic Sharne Rolfe is among the new wave of childcare professionals who acknowledge how important attachment is. Rolfe has worked hard to bring attachment theory insights to the training of childcare staff. Her excellent book attempts, rather optimistically, to find how it can be incorporated into daycare practice.

    Sharne Rolfe, *Rethinking Attachment for Early Childhood Practice*, Allen and Unwin, Sydney, 2004

14. Interviewed in M Bunting, 'Nursery Tales'

15. Harlow's powerful and haunting studies in the 1950s shaped modern thinking about parenthood. At the time he carried them out, it was still believed that affection weakened children and that physical contact of any kind should be kept to a minimum! With Renee Spitz, Anna

Freud and, later, Benjamin Spock, he made it respectable for parents in the modern world to cuddle their children.

Harry Harlow, 'Love in Infant Monkeys', *Scientific American*, 200, June 1959, 68, and at http://darkwing.uoregon.edu/~adoption/archive/Harlow LIM.htm

Chapter 4 – Your baby's growing brain

1. A N Schore, *Affect Regulation and the Origin of the Self: the neurobiology of emotional development*, Lawrence Erlbaum Associates, Hove, UK, 1994

    Schore himself spoke of the 'robust finding of elevated levels of aggression in children using centre care' and that 'such disturbing observations must be attended to very seriously'.

2. A N Schore, *Affect Regulation and Disorders of the Self*, Norton, 2003

3. A N Schore, *Affect Regulation and Repair of the Self*, Norton, 2003

    [Readers should note that the term 'affect' is used by scientists to denote 'emotions'. Showing warm emotions to another person is therefore 'affection'.]

4. The best popular coverage of Schore's work is Sue
    Gerhardt's beautiful book, *Why Love Matters: how affection
    shapes a baby's brain*, Brunner Routledge, Hove, 2004

    Some other books on brain development for general
    readership include:

    Stanley Greenspan, *Building Healthy Minds*, Perseus, New
    York, 1999

    Greenspan, America's most prominent neuroscientist, is
    notable for persuading parenting guru T Berry Brazelton
    to change his previously positive stance on daycare;
    together they published a book on this:

    T B Brazelton and S Greenspan, *The Irreducible Needs of
    Children: What every child must have to grow, learn and
    flourish*, Da Capo Press, New York, 2001

    Lise Eliot, *What's Going on in There?* Penguin, London,
    1999

    Eliot makes a powerful argument for knowing about
    brain development – 'Whether we realize it or not,
    almost every decision a parent makes boils down to a
    matter of our child's brain development, whether to have
    a glass of wine during pregnancy, whether to use drugs
    during childbirth, how long to breastfeed, how soon to
    return to work, whether to treat every ear infection,
    whether to enrol a child in a nursery, what kind of
    discipline to use, how much TV they should watch, and
    on and on.'

A and R Barnet, *The Youngest Minds*, Simon and Schuster, New York, 1998

Please note that I am not suggesting that any parent go out and read all these books. The central message of them all is that you would be better off spending this time visiting the beach or a park with your children!

5. Elinor Ames, Recommendations from the final report, 'The Development of Romanian Orphanage Children Adopted to Canada', 1997, cited in L Hanlon (ed.), *International Adoption, Challenges and Opportunities*, [publisher?], 1999

Chapter 5 – How babies teach us to parent

1. Psychiatrist Peter Cook believes daycare to be the greatest threat to our future mental health. In this erudite book he also dissects much of the current defence of daycare by US and Australian academia.

P Cook, *Early Childcare: Infants and Nations at Risk*, News Weekly Books, Melbourne, 1996

Chapter 6 – Babies and emotional intelligence

1. D Goleman, *Emotional Intelligence: Why it can matter more than IQ*, Bantam, UK, 2005

2. S Rolfe, B Nyland, and R Morda, 'Quality in Infant Care, observation on joint attention', *Australian Research in Early Childhood Education*, 2002, 9 (1), 86

This study reported that 'half the attempts at connection by the infants resulted in failure, interactions were fleeting, characterised by only one turn.'

Trudy Marshall, assistant director for daycare for a London borough, reported, after intensive observational studies, on what must have been some unusually grim London nurseries: 'the attention of adults flitted from child to child and rarely lasted more than thirty seconds with a single one ... To comfort a distressed child did not appear to play any part in the repertoire of adults in their daily care of children ... Signals of children's needs were missed, as were levels of distress and tiredness.'

T Marshall, cited in Buxton, *Ending the Mother War*, Pan Books, London, 1999

Chapter 7 – Why nursery doesn't work for babies

1. Rolfe, *Rethinking Attachment for Early Childhood Practice*

2. Doro Marden, 'Is recent research in the field of infant development and neuroscience relevant to the practice of psychotherapy?', unpublished MA dissertation, University of Middlesex

3. S Watamura and B Donzella, J Alwin and M Gunnar, 'Morning to afternoon increases in cortisol concentrations for infants and toddlers at a childcare centre, age differences and behavioural correlates', *Child Development*, 2003, 74 (4), 1006–20

4. R Lamb and L Ahnert, pre-publication release cited in L Ward, *Guardian*, 19 September 2005

Chapter 8 – Couples at the coalface

1. I am deeply indebted to the couples interviewed for this chapter, and also those whose stories were not used; all contributed to the thinking and conviction behind this book. Names and some details have been altered for privacy.

Chapter 9 – Our world of greed and speed

1. Professor Fiona Stanley, Australian of the Year for 2003, spent her year in that role highlighting the epidemic of mental health problems sweeping Western nations among the teenage and child-age groups. A good summary was given in her *ABC* interviews on 19 May and 6 October 2003, transcript at htttp://www.abc.net.au/enoughrope/stories/s961001.htm

2. The UK situation is summed up well in this article:

   J Carvel and R Smithers, 'Reforms pledged on mental health of children', *Guardian*, 14 September 2004

3. The article itself was based on a major review of national studies by S Collishaw, B Maughan, R Goodman and A Pickles in 'Time Trends in Adolescent Mental Health', *Journal of Child Psychology and Psychiatry*, November 2004, vol. 45, 8, 1350–62.

4. This comprehensive report, commissioned by the detergent multinational, predicted that on current trends 35 per cent of all Britons would be living alone by 2020. The largest growing group was people who had been in 'failed relationships'.

   Unilever, *Report on the UK Family*, 2005.

5. For example see:

   D Elkind, *The Hurried Child: growing up too fast too soon*, Da Capo Press, New York, 2001

6. Ralph Waldo Emerson put it this way: 'In dealing with my child, my Latin and my Greek, my accomplishments and my money stead me nothing; but as much soul as I have avails.'

Chapter 10 – A world where love can thrive

1. 'The number of Swedish babies in childcare fell from 3000 to 200 when paid parental leave was introduced.'

   Helen Wilkinson, *Time Out: the cost costs and benefits of paid parental leave*, Demos, London, 1997

2. Gerhardt, *Why Love Matters*

3. P Leach, *Children First*, Penguin, London, 1994

Acknowledgements

This book took a long time to write, and a lot of courage to publish. Wanda Whiteley, long-time editor of my books at HarperCollins, gave huge encouragement and practical help; she went beyond the scope of any editor I have known, organizing the interviews with UK parents and helping to overcome my Australian conceptions of the English! Wanda could easily have been listed as co-author by the time it was complete. Carole Tonkinson took over the very final stage and brought it home. Matthew Cory in England and Sean Doyle in Australia sub-edited patiently and with a light hand. David Hancock took over 200 superb and sometimes shattering photos of what life is really like in daycare, using some of the best crèches in Sydney, Australia as his subject. (A DVD featuring these photographs with narration by the author is planned for 2006.)

Shaaron Biddulph showed me over a period of 20 years what real mothering looks like, and along with many mothers I have admired and watched in action, she helped me realize what a deficient and sad substitute group care is for what nature intended for tiny babies and toddlers.

Rohan Biddulph and Vanessa Warren read early drafts and were encouraging and helpful. Ariana Biddulph kept my feet truly on the ground. Doro Marden was a wonderful source of intelligence, perspective and urging on. The women of the Meander Valley said 'get on with it' while sharpening my thinking; and my four sisters-in-law – Kerry Pickett, Vicki Giarraputo, Lindy Shillito and Jenny Matthewson – gave me insider feedback from their respective child development professions. Researcher and academic writer Ian Ochiltree gave cogent and thoughtful advice throughout.

Anne Manne, one of Australia's most respected researchers on parenthood, released her book *Motherhood* in 2005, breaking the ice on this topic, and setting such an example of scholarship, sensitivity and richness of material that I felt happy to be in the same team. Anne's research and personal support was very helpful, as was the written work of Sue Gerhardt, Jay Belsky, and the amazing work of Allan Schore, in putting into clear technical detail what my over-sized heart was telling me was true.

About the author

Steve Biddulph was born in the 1950s in Yorkshire, the then 'world capital of negative parenting'. As a young psychologist in the 1970s, he studied families and parenting in New Guinea, Calcutta, and the United States, and was a pioneer of family therapy in Australia.

Steve's simple but powerful books are today found in 27 languages and over four million homes worldwide. He is especially known for raising the profile and importance of fathering, and promoting a more positive and proactive approach to the raising and education of boys.

For the last four years, Steve has worked supporting campaigns to end the Australian government's maltreatment of refugee parents and children in detention centres in remote desert locations. In 2005, this campaigning by thousands of Australians lead to the release of almost all families from detention.

He lives on a small permaculture property with his wife, daughter, and a series of recovering wombats.

Index

Printed by RR Donnelley at Glasgow, UK